PRIMARY MATHEMATICS

2B

Home Instructor's Guide

Authored by: Jennifer Hoerst
Printed by: Avyx, Inc.

Go to:
www.avyx.com

Or e-mail:
info@avyx.dom

Or write:
Avyx, Inc.
8032 South Grant Way
Littleton, CO 80122-2705
USA
303-483-0140

ISBN 13: 978-1-887840-60-6
ISBN: 1-887840-60-5

Printed in the United States of America

Preface and General Instructions

This guide is meant to help instructors using *Primary Mathematics 2B* when teaching one student or a small group of students. It should be used as a guide and adapted as needed. It contains

 objectives,

 notes to the instructor, providing added explanation of concepts,

 instructional ideas and suggested activities,

 and ideas for games

to reinforce concepts from the

 corresponding textbook pages, learning tasks, and

 "homework" assignments.

Included is a <u>suggested</u> weekly schedule and pages for mental math (in the appendix). The schedule is simply to help you keep on track – you need to spend more time on a topic if necessary and less time if your student is proficient in the topic. Practices and reviews in the text are scheduled as they are encountered, and can be done independently by the student, or can be used as part of a lesson. Since some of the practice questions are challenging, they provide good opportunities for discussion. When there are several practices one after the other, you may want to go on to the next topic and insert the rest of the practices later to allow for more ongoing review. The mental math pages can be used as worksheets and many can also be done orally, with your student seeing the problem and answering out loud rather than writing the answer down. They can be used any time after they are referenced in this guide, and can be used more than once for more practice. So if four Mental Math pages are listed for one lesson, they are not meant to all be done during that lesson, but can be used any time after that lesson for review and mental math practice.

Answers to the workbook exercises are given at the end of this guide.

This guide can be used with both the third edition and the U.S. edition of *Primary Mathematics 2A*.

3d› indicates portions pertaining only to the third edition, and

US› indicates portions pertaining only to the US edition (except for number words).

U.S. spellings and conventions will be used in this guide. Answers involving number words will use the current U.S. convention of reserving the word "and" for the decimal and not using it in number words for whole numbers.

Contents

Answers to Mental Math

Appendix

Suggested Weekly Schedule

WB: Workbook   TB: Textbook

	Part	Lesson	Text pages	Exercises	Materials	Mental Math
1	**Unit 1 Addition and Subtraction**					
	1 Finding the Missing Number	(1) Missing Part	6-8		Small objects Index card	
		(2) Missing Whole	8-9	WB Ex. 1		
		(3) Make 100	9-10	WB Ex. 2	Hundred chart	Mental Math 1
		(4) Practice	11	TB Practice 1A	Dice	Mental Math 2
2	2 Methods for Mental Addition	(1) Add Ones or Tens	12-13	WB Ex. 3	Number discs	Mental Math 3 Mental Math 4
		(2) Add Ones, Tens, or Hundreds	13	WB Ex. 4		Mental Math 5 Mental Math 6
		(3) Add 2-Digit Numbers	13	WB Ex. 5	Hundred chart Counters Number cards	Mental Math 7
		(4) Add 98 or 99	14	WB Ex. 6 WB Ex. 7	Base-10 blocks Number cards Dice	Mental Math 8 Mental Math 9
3	3 Methods for Mental Subtraction	(1) Subtract Ones or Tens	15-16	WB Ex. 8	Number discs	Mental Math 10
		(2) Subtract Ones, Tens, or Hundreds	16	WB Ex. 9		Mental Math 11 Mental Math 12
		(3) Subtract 2-Digit Numbers	16	WB Ex. 10	Hundred chart Counters Number cards	Mental Math 13
		(4) Subtract 98 or 99 I	17	WB Ex. 11	Base-10 blocks Base-10 blocks	
4		(5) Subtract 98 or 99 II	17	WB Ex. 12	Number cards Dice	Mental Math 14
		(6) Practice	18	TB Practice 1B		Mental Math 15
		(7) Practice	19	TB Practice 1C		Mental Math 16 Mental Math 17
	Review			WB Review 1		
5	**Unit 2 Multiplication and Division**					
	1 Multiplying and Dividing by 4	(1) Counting by Fours	20-21	WB Ex 13	Multilink cubes	
		(2) Related Facts	22-23	WB Ex. 14 WB Ex. 15		Mental Math 18
		(3) Word Problems		WB Ex. 16 WB Ex. 17	Fact cards, Dice Number cards	Mental Math 19 Mental Math 20
		(4) Division by 4	23-24	WB Ex. 18, #1-2	Counters	
		(5) Division Facts			Number cards Fact cards Counters Hundred chart	Mental Math 21
6		(6) Word Problems	24	WB Ex. 18, #3-5	Counters	
		(7) Practice	25	TB Practice 2A		
	2 Multiplying and Dividing by 5	(1) Counting by Fives	26-28	WB Ex. 19	Hundred chart	Mental Math 22

	Part	Lesson	Text pages	Exercises	Materials	Mental Math
		(2) Multiplication Facts	28	WB Ex. 20	Linking cubes	Mental Math 23 Mental Math 24
		(3) Division by 5	28	WB Ex. 21		Mental Math 25
		(4) Word Problems	29	TB Practice 2B		
7	3 Multiplying and Dividing by 10	(1) Multiplication by 10	30-31	WB Ex. 22		Mental Math 26
		(2) Division by 10	31	WB Ex. 23		
		(3) Practice	32-34	TB Practice 2C TB Practice 2D TB Practice 2E		Mental Math 27 Mental Math 28
	Review		35	TB Review A WB Review 2		
8	**Unit 3 Money**					
	1 Dollars and Cents	(1) Dollars and Cents	36-37	WB Ex. 24	Coins and bills	
		(2) Writing Money Amounts	37	WB Ex. 25 WB Ex. 26		
		(3) Converting Money	38-39			
		(4) Changing Dollars and Cents	39	WB Ex. 27		
		(5) Making Change for $1	40	WB Ex. 28		
		(6) Making Change for $5 or $10	40	WB Ex. 29		
9		(7) Word Problems	41	TB Practice 3A WB Ex. 30	Store cards Coins and bills	
	2 Adding Money	(1) Adding Cents or Dollars	43	WB Ex. 31		
		(2) Adding Cents and Dollars	42-43	WB Ex. 32		
		(3) Adding Money	44	WB Ex. 33		
		(4) Mental Math	44	WB Ex. 34		Mental Math 29
		(5) Word Problems	45		Store cards	
10	3 Subtracting Money	(1) Subtracting Cents or Dollars	47	WB Ex. 35	Coins and bills	
		(2) Subtracting Cents and Dollars	46-47	WB Ex. 36		
		(3) Subtracting Money	48	WB Ex. 37		
		(4) Mental Math	48	WB Ex. 38		
11		(5) Word Problems	49	WB Ex. 39	Store cards	
		(6) Practice	50-51	TB Practice 3B TB Practice 3B		
	Review		50-51	WB Review 3 WB Review 4		
12	**Unit 4 Fractions**					
	1 Halves and Quarters	(1) Halves and Quarters	52-53	WB Ex. 40	Sheets of paper	
	2 Writing Fractions	(1) Fractional Notation	54-55	WB Ex. 41	Fraction circles and bars	
		(2) Writing Fractions	56	WB Ex. 42 WB Ex. 43		
		(3) Comparing Fractions	57	WB Ex. 44	Fraction circles and bars	
		(4) Making a Whole	57	WB Ex. 45	Fraction cards	

	Part	Lesson	Text pages	Exercises	Materials	Mental Math
13	Review		58-59	TB Review B TB Review C		
	Unit 5 Time					
	1 Telling Time	(1) Time to 5-Minutes	60-62	WB Ex. 46	clock	
		(2) Time of Day	63	WB Ex. 47		
	2 Time Intervals	(1) Time Intervals	64-67	WB Ex. 48		
14		(2) Start and End Times	67	WB Ex. 49		
		(3) Practice	68	TB Practice 5A		
	Review		69	TB Review D WB Review 5		
	Unit 6 Capacity					
	1 Comparing Capacity	(1) Comparing Capacity	70-71	WB Ex. 50 WB Ex. 51	Containers	
	2 Liters	(1) Liters	72-75	**US**›WB Ex. 52 **3d**›WB Ex. 52 **3d**›WB Ex. 53	Liter measure	
15		(2) Word Problems	76	TB Practice 6A **US**›WB Ex. 53 **3d**›WB Ex. 54		
	US› 3 Gallons, Quarts, Pints and Cups	(1) Gallons, Quarts, Pints and Cups	**US**›77-80	**US**›WB Ex. 54	Quart measure Containers	
	Review		**US**›81 **3d**›77	TB Review E		
	Unit 7 Graphs					
	1 Picture Graphs	(1) Picture Graphs I	**US**›82-85 **3d**›78-81	WB Ex. 55 WB Ex. 56	Counters Linking cubes	
		(2) Picture Graphs II	**US**›86-87 **3d**›82-83	WB Ex. 57 WB Ex. 58		
16	Review		**US**›88-89 **3d**›84-85	TB Review F TB Review G		
	Unit 8 Geometry					
	1 Flat and Curved Faces	(1) Faces and Shapes	**US**›90-92 **3d**›86-88	WB Ex. 59	objects of various shapes	
	2 Making Shapes	(1) Combining Shapes	**US**›93-95 **3d**›89-91	WB Ex. 61 WB Ex. 62		
		(2) Curves	**US**›96-97 **3d**›92-93	WB Ex. 62 WB Ex. 63		
17		(3) Patterns	**US**›98-99 **3d**›94-95	WB Ex. 64		
	Review		**US**›100-101 **3d**›96-97	TB Review H WB Review 6		
	Unit 9 Area					
	1 Square Units	(1) Area I **US**› **3d**›	102-104 99-100	WB Ex. 65	cut squares graph paper	
		(2) Area II **US**› **3d**›	105 101	WB Ex. 66 WB Ex. 67		
18	Review		**US**›106-112 **3d**›102-104	TB Review I TB Review J ‹**US** WB Review 7 WB Review 8		

Additional Materials

Base-10 set. A set usually has 100 unit-cubes, 10 or more ten-rods, 10 hundred-flats, and 1 thousand-block.

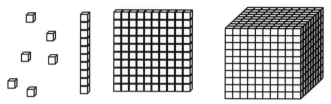

Number discs. Use plastic or cardboard discs and write "1000" on a few, "100" on twenty discs, "10" on twenty discs, and "1" on twenty discs.

Multilink Cubes or Connect-a-Cubes
These are cubes, usually measuring about three-quarters of an inch or 2 cm, which can link to each other on all six sides.

Hundred chart Make one or buy one with squares large enough to cover with counters or coins.

Counters (plastic discs) or **coins**.

Clock with geared hands.

Graph paper

Index cards, dice

1	2	3	4	5	6	7	8	9	10
11	12	13	14	15	16	17	18	19	20
21	22	23	24	25	26	27	28	29	30
31	32	33	34	35	36	37	38	39	40
41	42	43	44	45	46	47	48	49	50
51	52	53	54	55	56	57	58	59	60
61	62	63	64	65	66	67	68	69	70
71	72	73	74	75	76	77	78	79	80
81	82	83	84	85	86	87	88	89	90
91	92	93	94	95	96	97	98	99	100

Plastic 1-liter/1-quart measuring cup.

Number cards. 4 sets of cards with the numbers 0-9. You can use a deck of playing cards, remove the face cards, white out the Ace and write a 1, and white out the 1 and the symbols on the "10" cards.

Money, either play or real or a combination, of all denominations up to $10, including three $10 bills.

Store cards. Pictures of items with cost, from $0.01 to $10.00. Cut pictures from magazines, newspaper ads, coupons, etc. and glue to index cards. Add a cost, using decimal notation, e.g., $4.60. About half should be costs below $1, and another half costs between $1 and $10.

Unit 1 – Addition and Subtraction

Part 1 – Finding the Missing Number

(1) Missing Number (pp. 6-9)

➢ Find the missing part in addition and subtraction equations.
➢ Find the missing whole in a subtraction equation.

In *Primary Mathematics 1*, addition and subtraction were associated with the part-whole concept of number bonds.

When we know the parts, we use **addition** to find the whole. This can be represented as a number bond with a missing total.

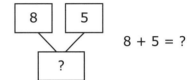

This can also be represented pictorially.

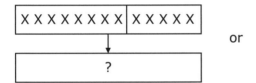

or

When we know the whole and one of the parts of the whole, we use **subtraction** to find the missing part. This can be represented as a number bond with a missing part.

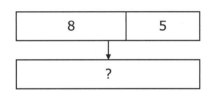

This can also be represented pictorially:

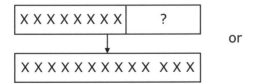

or

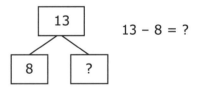

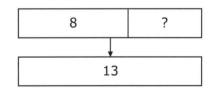

In this section, your student will use the part-whole concept to find a missing number in addition and subtraction equations:

- In the equation **? + 8 = 13** the missing number represents an unknown part. The unknown part can therefore be found by subtraction: **13 – 8 = ?.**

- In the equation **13 - ? = 8** the whole is given, an unknown part is removed, leaving a known part. Since we have a whole and a known part, the unknown part can be found by subtraction: **13 – 8 = ?**.
- In the equation **? - 8 = 5**, the whole is unknown. When one part is subtracted from the whole, the result is the other part. Since we have two parts, the unknown whole can be found by addition: **8 + 5 = ?**.

If your student has done earlier levels of Primary Mathematics, she will probably be able to solve the missing number problems in this section using mental calculations; otherwise she can use the addition or subtraction algorithm.

Part + ? = Whole
Whole - ? = Part
? – Part = Part

Take your time with these first two lessons. It may take more than one or two days to be sure your student understands the concepts.

➤ Review number bonds and the concept of finding a missing part whole of a number bond using addition, and a missing part using subtraction. Draw some number bonds with missing part or missing whole and have your student write an equation and solve.

➤ Use small **objects**, such as unit cubes from a base-10 set, or pennies, and an **index card**. Put 11 down in a row and cover 4 with a card. Put another 11 down in a row below it.

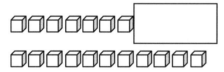

Write the equations

7 + _____ = 11   and   _____ + 7 = 11.

Tell your student that both rows have the same number. The second row has the total, the first has one part showing, and one part covered. Ask him which part corresponds to the 11 in the equation, and which part corresponds to the 7.

The covered part is the amount that goes in the blank line. 11 is the whole, and 7 is one part. Draw the number bond. How do we find the other part? We can use subtraction. Write the equation.

7 + _____ = 11 is the same as 11 – 7 = _____

Now discuss a situation where we start with 11 objects, and take some away, so that we are left with 7 objects. We know the whole, and one part. Ask your student which number is the whole, and which is the part. Draw the number bond. Ask him how we can find the other part? We can subtract.

11 – _____ = 7 is the same as 11 – 7 = _____

Pages 6-7
Learning Tasks 1-2(b), pp. 7-8

5
1. **8**   (20 – 12 = 8)
2. (a) **16**   (30 – 14 =6)
    (b) **16**   (21 – 5 = 16)

➤ Repeat with other examples such as:

23 + _____ = 37   ↔   37 – 23 = _____   (14)

_____ + 42 = 60   ↔   60 – 42 = _____   (18)

76 – _____ = 4   ↔   76 – 4 = _____   (72)

In each case, we know the whole and a part, and need to find another part. If it helps, draw some models to illustrate. Do not require your student to draw pictorial models at this stage.

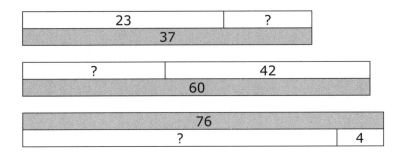

➤ Try some examples within 1000. You can use this as an opportunity to review the subtraction algorithm.

486 + _____ = 925   ↔   925 – 486 = _____   (439)

$$\begin{array}{r} {}^{8}\,{}^{1}1 \\ \cancel{9}\,\cancel{2}\,{}^{1}5 \\ -\ 4\ 8\ 6 \\ \hline 4\ 3\ 9 \end{array}$$

(2) Missing Whole (pp. 8-9)

 ➢ Find the missing whole in a subtraction equation.

➤ Put blocks or **objects** in two rows, as before, but cover up the whole with an index card or paper:

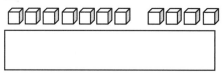

Tell your student that we have a certain number of objects, and take away 7. There are 4 left. Or we take away 4, and there are 7 left.
Write the equations

_____ – 4 = 7   and   _____ – 7 = 4

We know both parts, but not the whole amount we started with. How do we find the whole? We add.

_____ – 4 = 7 is the same as

4 + 7 = _____

Repeat with other examples such as:

_____ – 24 = 48   ↔   24 + 48 = _____   (72)

_____ – 2 = 88   ↔   88 + 2 = _____   (90)

In each case, we need to find the whole.

?	
24	48

 Learning Tasks 2(c)-3, pp. 8-9

In 2(c), point out that we know both parts, but not the whole. Whenever we see a subtraction equation where the first term is unknown, it must be an unknown whole, since in subtraction we are taking a part away from the whole. For task 3, your student should be able to look at the equation and determine whether she needs to subtract or add the two given numbers to get the missing number. Do not require your student to write the related equation if she can solve the problem without writing it down. If, on the other hand, she is having trouble solving these, have her write an empty number bond and try to determine which number goes in which part, and then write the related equation.

2. (c) 24   (18 + 6 = 24)

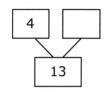

3. (a) 4 + ___ = 13 We are given a part and a whole.
   We subtract.   13 – 4 = **9**

   (b) 20 – ___ = 13   We are given a whole and a part. We subtract.
   20 – 13 = **7**

   (c) 9 + ___ = 39   We are given a part and a whole. We subtract.
   39 – 9 = **30**

   (d) 47 – ___ = 19   We are given a whole and a part. We subtract.
   47 – 19 = **28**

   (e) ___ + 8 = 15   We are given a part and a whole. We subtract.
   15 – 8 = **7**

   (f) ___ – 7 = 10   We are given the two parts. We add.
   10 + 7 = **17**

   (g) ___ + 14 = 60   We are given a part and a whole. We subtract.
   60 – 14 = **46**

   (h) ___ – 16 = 40   We are given the two parts. We add.
   40 + 16 = **56**

 Workbook Exercise 1

➤ Coded number puzzles can be used to find a missing addend and apply concepts of addition and subtraction. In them, digits are replaced by a symbol or letter. If the same symbol or letter appears more than once in the problem, it represents the same number. Number puzzles are common in problem solving books and you can make them up yourself. Your student may be interested in trying them. Here are a few:

```
      &  &  3
  +   ?  2  &
  %   2  ?  8
```
Since 3 + 5 = 8, the & must be 5. Replace the other &s with 5. The ? then must be 7. Replace those. The % must be 1.

```
      2  @  9
  +   #  #  4
      @  0  #
```
The # must be 3. The 10 is renamed. Replace the #s with 3, and write a 1 above the @. Now you have 1 + @ + 3 = 0. Since it can't equal 0, it must be 10. @ must therefore be 6.

```
      3  5  A
  -   B  C  9
      C  C  7
```
Since 7 is smaller than 9, the problem must require renaming.   - 9 = 7 is the same as 9 + 7 = ___ . So ___ is 16, and A is 6. Cross out the 5 and replace with 4. The only possibility for C is 2. So B must be 1.

(3) Make 100 (pp. 9-10)

> ➤ Use the "count-on" strategy to make 100.
> ➤ Use the missing number strategy to make 100.
> ➤ Mentally subtract from 100.

In this section, your student will learn two strategies for finding the missing part when the total is 100.

Learning Task 4 on p. 9 illustrates one strategy for making 100 involving using the idea of counting on:

$$68 + \underline{} = 100$$

$$68 \xrightarrow{+2} 70 \xrightarrow{+30} 100$$

Count on ones from 68 to 70, and then count on tens from 70 to 100. 32 more are needed. You can also count on tens from 68 and then ones from 98 to 100:

$$68 \xrightarrow{+30} 98 \xrightarrow{+2} 100$$

Learning Task 5 on p. 10 illustrates a second strategy, which is to use the knowledge that 100 is 9 tens and 10 ones to find the answer.

$$53 + \underline{} = 100$$

```
  5 tens   3 ones            5 tens   3 ones
+    tens     ones   ⟶    + 4 tens   7 ones
  9 tens  10 ones            9 tens  10 ones
```

Learning Task 4, p. 9

Use a grid of 100 square units such as a **hundred chart** or a 100 flat from a **base-10 set**. Write the equation

$$68 + \underline{} = 100$$

Cover up 68 square units. Ask how many are covered. Show that the other part can be found by first adding ones (2) to get a ten, and then adding tens (30) to get to 100. Ask your student if he sees any other way to do it. We can count by tens first to 98, and then by ones to 100. Repeat with other examples, if necessary.

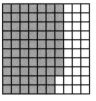

Write the equation

68 + _____ = 100

Remind your student that we have a whole, and one part, so this can also be written:

100 − 53 = _____

Cover up the square units again so that the partially covered column is the last column. Explain that 100 is 9 tens and 10 ones. 6 tens are covered, so 3 more tens are needed to make 9 tens. 8 ones are covered, so 2 more ones are needed to make 10 ones. There are 3 tens and 2 ones, or 32 squares, uncovered. Repeat with other examples, if necessary. To find the answer, your student must make a nine with the tens of the given number, and a ten with the ones of the given number.

 Learning Tasks 5-7, p. 10

5.   **47**

6.   (a) **66**   (b) **24**
     (c) **18**   (d) **91**

7.   (a) **74**   (b) **39**   (c) **58**
     (d) **4**   (e) **98**   (f) **92**

 Workbook Exercise 2

(4) Practice (p. 11)

➢ Find the missing number in addition and subtraction equations.
➢ Review word problems involving addition and subtraction.

Strategies for solving word problems were covered in *Primary Mathematics 2A*. Your student should determine whether the problem gives a whole and a part, and asks for a missing part, or whether the problem gives two parts, and asks for a whole, or total.

Students can do this practice with you as a lesson, or independently. You may want to review word problems with your student using the problems in Practice 1A. Ask your student pertinent questions, such as, "Does the problem give you a total amount? What is it?"

Your student is not required to use mental math to solve all the word problems in this and the other practices. She should learn to determine when mental math is appropriate, or when it might be better to use the addition or subtraction algorithm (rewriting the problem vertically, and adding or subtracting starting from the lowest place value, renaming as necessary). The word problems are a review of material learned in earlier levels of *Primary Mathematics*, as well as concepts learned in this particular unit.

Practice 1A, p. 11

1. (a) **15**   (b) **17**   (c) **39**   (d) **22**
   (e) **14**   (f) **90**   (g) **54**   (h) **72**
   (i) **75**   (j) **7**   (k) **37**   (l) **43**

2. (a) **62**   (b) **1**   (c) **2**
   (d) **96**   (e) **91**   (f) **97**

3. 215 - _____ = 36
   Use subtraction: 215 - 36 = 179
   He sold **179** ducks.

number of ducks: 215	
number sold: ?	number left: 36

4. _____ - $127 = $53
   Use addition: $127 + $53 = $180
   He had **$180** at first.

total money: ?	
cost of fan: $127	money left: $53

5. (a) 324 g - 86 g = 238 g
      Weight of the cucumber = **238 g**

cabbage: 324 g	
cucumber: 86 g	?

   (b) 238 g + 324 g = 562 g
      Total weight = **562 g**

cucumber: 86 g	cabbage: 324 g
total weight ?	

➤ Label two **dice** with stickers, one with the numbers 1-6, and the other with the numbers 4-9. Roll the dice. Allow the student to pick one to be the tens and the other to be ones. For example, if a 6 and a 2 is rolled the number can be 62 or 26. Your student must give the number that makes 100 with this number.

➤ Draw a picture of squares in the shape of a cross. Write down a set of 5 numbers. 4 of them should be pairs that make 100, and the fifth a random number, for example, give him the numbers 45, 62, 23, 55, and 38. (45 and 55, 62 and 38) Ask your student to place the numbers in the cross so that the sum of the numbers across is the same as the sum of the numbers down. If he has trouble, tell him that there are two pairs that make 100 and see if he can find them. Help him see that they can go on the arms, and the fifth number in the middle. Repeat with other combinations.

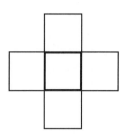

➤ Use Mental Math worksheets 1-2 for extra practice

Part 2 – Methods for Mental Addition

 Mental Math strategies are reviewed in this section, and new ones are introduced. Your student may already be using some of the new strategies.

Learning and using mental calculation strategies encourages flexibility in thinking about numbers and helps the student develop a strong number sense. Flexibility is a key here. Though the students are taught strategies, they should be encouraged to develop, utilize, and share their own strategies.

The following strategies will be reviewed or taught here. The illustrations are included here to help make the strategies clearer with respect to place values to you as the teacher — your student is not going to be drawing these illustrations.

➢ Add 1, 2, or 3 by counting on.
   338 + 3 = 341; count on 339, 340, 341

➢ Add a 1-digit number to a 2-digit or 3-digit number without renaming by adding ones to ones.
   155 + 4 = 159

➢ Add 10, 20, or 30 by counting on.
   288 + 30 = 318; count up 298, 308, 318 (or count tens first then add ones: 29, 30, 31 tens, 318.

➢ Add tens to each other without renaming by adding the tens.
   150 + 30 = 180

➢ Add tens to a 2-digit or 3-digit number without renaming by adding to the tens.
   155 + 40 = 195

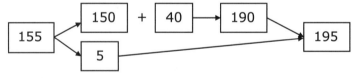

➢ Add a 1-digit number to a 2-digit or 3-digit number by making a 10:

   176 + 8 = 184

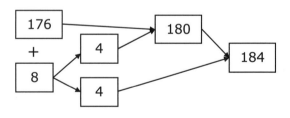

➢ Add a 1-digit number to a 2-digit or 3-digit number by recalling the addition fact and renaming ten ones as a ten.
   176 + 8 = 184

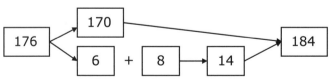

- ➢ Add tens to a 2-digit or 3-digit number by adding the tens using the same strategies as if they were ones.
     283 + 70 = 353 (28 + 7 = 35)

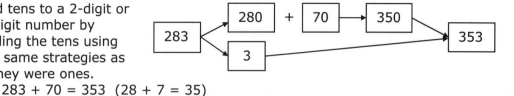

- ➢ Add hundreds to a 3-digit number by adding hundreds to hundreds.
     234 + 500 = 734

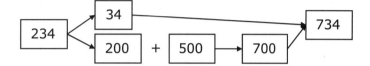

- ➢ Add two 2-digit numbers by first finding the tens and then the ones.
     53 + 34 = 87

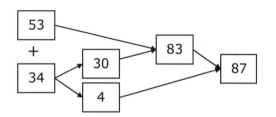

- ➢ Add a number close to 100 by making 100. (This is the method shown in the text.)
     457 + 98 = 555

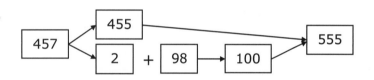

- ➢ Add a number close to 100 by first adding 100 and then subtracting the difference. (This is easier to do than making 100.)
     457 + 98 = 457 + 100 – 2 = 557 – 2 = 555

Your student may be able to extend the strategies given in this section or derive other strategies. Do not discourage any attempts to manipulate numbers. Do not require him to write down his steps, or explain his steps in writing. This negates the usefulness of mental math. Encourage him to share his ideas and methods orally. If he gives a wrong answer, help him to go through his process step by step to try to find the error. However, do not require him to use mental calculations in problems where he is more comfortable using the addition algorithm. He should find out for himself when and where to try mental math, and also when it is safer for him to stick to the standard addition algorithm.

(1) Add Ones or Tens (pp. 12-13)

➢   Add ones, tens, or hundreds to a 3-digit number when there is no renaming.
➢   Add ones or tens to a 2-digit number.

Page 12

Illustrate the concepts on this page with actual **number discs**, base-10 blocks, or other base-10 material, if necessary. A suggested procedure is given below. In your discussion, emphasize the place value of the numbers. For example, call 20 "2 tens" to emphasize that it is added to the number in the tens place.

Set out 3 hundreds, 5 tens, and 6 ones.

Write: 356

Say: This is 3 hundreds, 5 tens, 6 ones. How do we know it is 5 tens? (because of the place 5 is in)

Ask: What number is 2 ones more than 356?

Add 2 ones to the ones. Count on by ones. 356, 357, 358.

Write: 356 + 2 = 358

The 2 is being added to the 6; they are both ones.

Ask: What number is 2 tens more than 358?

Add 2 tens to the tens. Count on by tens. 358, 368, 378.

Write: 358 + 20 = 378

The 2 is being added to the 5; they are both tens.

Ask: What number is 2 hundreds more than 378?

Add 2 hundreds to the 3. Count on by hundreds. 378, 478, 578.

Write: 378 + 200 = 578

The 2 is being added to the 3; they are both hundreds.

➤ Use **number discs** to illustrate the addition of ones to a 2-digit number. Set out 5 tens and 4 ones. Add 8 more ones next to them. Write 54 + 8 = ? and discuss strategies to mentally find the value of 54 + 8. Explain that in using mental strategies we often start at the highest place value.

$$54 + 8 = \mathbf{6}\_$$

o   Find the tens: Before determining the tens for the answer, look to the ones. Will the ones increase the tens? Yes, so add 1 to the tens. The tens of the sum will be 6. Write 6 for the tens.

o   Find the ones: Discuss two methods.

  1. Use the addition fact (4 + 8 = 12). This tells us there are 2 ones. To show this, move the 4 ones over to the right with the other ones, and then change 10 ones for a ten. You can also draw a number bond picture.

$$54 + 8 = 50 + 12 = 62$$
$$50 \quad 4$$

  2. Make a ten (54 takes 6 from 8 to make 60, there are 2 left over). Show this by moving 6 of the ones over towards the 54, and then changing 10 ones for a ten. You can also draw a number bond.

$$54 + 8 = 60 + 2 = 62$$
$$6 \quad 2$$

        Write 2 for the ones.

$$54 + 8 = 6\mathbf{2}$$

Write the problem 29 + 2. Tell your student that if she is adding a small number such as 1, 2, or 3, she can simply count on: 30, 31. She should realize that when counting on from 29 not to include 29.

$$29 + 2 = 31$$

Write the problem 55 + 4. Ask your student to look at the ones. 5 and 4 are not enough to make another ten. The tens digit stays the same, and the ones are simply added together.

$$55 + 4 = 59$$

➤ Illustrate the addition of tens to a 2-digit number. Display 4 tens and 5 ones. Add 8 more tens next to them. Write 45 + 80 = ? and discuss strategies to mentally find the value of 45 + 80

○ Add the tens. We can add the tens by just adding the digits. Since 4 + 8 = 12, then 4 tens + 8 tens = 12 tens. Write 12 tens.

○ Find the ones: The ones are just the 5 from 45. Write 5 down for ones.

You can show the process with number bonds.

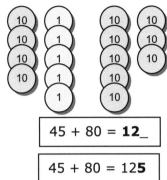

45 + 80 = **12**_

45 + 80 = 12**5**

$$45 + 80 = 120 + 5 = 125$$
5   40

Write the problem 91 + 20. Tell your student that if he is adding 10, 20, or 30, he can simply count on by tens: 101, 111.

91 + 20 = 111

➤ Mental Math 3 and 4 can be used for extra practice now or later.

 Learning Task 1, p. 13

1. (a) **49**   (b) **45**   (c) **61**
    (d) **50**   (e) **90**   (f) **140**
    (g) **54**   (h) **93**   (i) **147**

 Workbook Exercise 3

(2) Add Ones, Tens, or Hundreds (p. 13)

 ➢ Add ones, tens, or hundreds to a 3-digit number.

➤ Use **number discs** to illustrate mental addition of ones to a 3-digit number where there is renaming. Set out 3 hundreds, 5 tens, and 6 ones. Set out another 8 ones. Discuss strategies to mentally find the sum for 356 + 8.

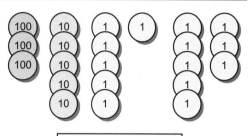

- o   Find the hundreds. Since we won't be adding tens, the hundreds stay the same. Write 3 for the hundreds.
- o   Add 56 + 8 using the same strategies already discussed. Write down the tens and then the ones.

You can draw a number bond to illustrate the process.

$$356 + 8 = \mathbf{3}\_\_$$

$$356 + 8 = 3\mathbf{6}\_$$

$$356 + 8 = 36\mathbf{4}$$

$$356 + 8 = 300 + 56 + 8 = 364$$

300   56

➤ Illustrate mental addition of tens to a 3-digit number where there is renaming. Start with the original 3 hundreds, 5 tens, and 6 ones. Set out another 8 tens. Discuss strategies to mentally find the sum for 356 + 80.

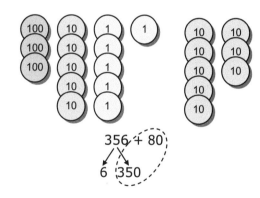

- o   Since we are adding tens, we can ignore the ones for now. You can show the number bond.
- o   350 is 35 tens. We can add 35 tens and 8 tens using the same strategies for adding 35 ones and 8 ones. Ask for the sum of 35 and 8 (35 + 8 = 43). If 35 + 8 = 43, then 35 tens + 8 tens = 43 tens. Write down 43 tens.
- o   Find the ones. The ones will just be the 6 from 356. Write 6 down for the ones.

356 + 80

6   350

$$356 + 80 = \mathbf{43}\_$$

$$356 + 80 = 43\mathbf{6}$$

$$356 + 80 = 350 + 80 + 6 = 436$$

6   350

Write another problem such as 479 + 30.
Explain that with smaller tens we can
count up: 48 tens, 49 tens, 50 tens, so
the answer is 50 tens and nine, or 509.

479 + 30 = 509

 You can use Mental Math 5 and 6 for more practice.

 Learning Task 2, p. 13

2. (a) **162**   (b) **283**   (c) **612**
    (d) **380**   (e) **305**   (f) **214**
    (g) **400**   (h) **800**   (i) **900**
    (j) **456**   (k) **804**   (l) **965**

Workbook Exercise 4

(3) Add 2-Digit Numbers (p. 13)

 ➢ Add 2-digit numbers mentally.

 Use number discs to illustrate mental addition of 2-digit numbers. Discuss methods to add 36 and 45 mentally:

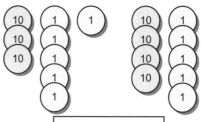

1. Find each digit from left to right:
   - Find the tens. Look ahead to the ones – will adding the ones increase the tens? Yes, so add the tens and increase the sum by 1. Write 8 for the tens.
   - Find the ones: 6 + 5 = 11, so the ones is 1. Write 1 for the ones.
2. Find an intermediate number.
   - Add the tens of the second number to the first number to get the intermediate sum 76.
   - Add the ones to get the final sum. 76 + 5 = 81.

| 36 + 45 = ? |
| 36 + 45 = **8**_ |
| 36 + 45 = 8**1** |

$$36 \xrightarrow{+40} 76 \xrightarrow{+5} 81$$

36 + 45 = 81

 Use Mental Math 7 for additional practice.

 Learning Task 3-4, p. 13

3. **69**

4. (a) **69**   (b) **77**   (c) **88**
   (d) **79**   (e) **79**   (f) **59**

 Material: A **hundred chart** for each player, **counters** or coins, different for each player, four sets of **number cards** from 0-9 and four extra 0 cards. Procedure: Shuffle the cards and set them face down. Players take turns drawing 4 cards and arranging them into two numbers less than 100. If 0 is drawn, it can be used as a ten to make a 1-digit number; otherwise both numbers are 2-digit numbers. For example, 3, 6, 4, and 0 are drawn. The numbers could be 36 and 40, 34 and 60, 4 and 63, etc. The player adds the numbers mentally and covers up the answer on the hundred chart with a counter or coin. If the sum is more than 99 he needs to rearrange the numbers to two different 2-digit numbers. The first player to get 3 in a row wins.

 Workbook Exercise 5

(4) Add 98 or 99 (p. 14)

 ➢ Add 98 or 99 mentally.

➤ Use **base-10 blocks**. Set out a number such as 242. Place a 100-flat below it and cover up one square.

Write: 242 + 99

Ask your student how she can use the idea of making 100 to add 99.

➢ She can take 1 from 242, and add that to 99 to make 100.

➢ She can count on by 100, and then back 1.
$$242 + 99 = 242 + 100 - 1$$
$$= 342 - 1$$
$$= 341$$
242, 342, 341

$$242 + 99$$
241   1
241   100
341

Now write: 242 + 98

Ask her for ways to add 98 mentally.

➢ She can make 100 (shown at right).

➢ She can also count up 100, and then count back 2

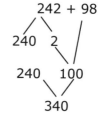

$$242 + 98$$
240   2
240   100
340

$$242 + 98 = 242 + 100 - 2$$
$$= 342 - 2$$
$$= 340$$
242, 342, 340

Repeat with 242 + 97. Count up 100, and back 3. 242 + 97 = 339

 Learning Tasks 5-9, p. 14

5. **103**

6. (a) **101**   (b) **108**   (c) **103**
    (d) **145**   (e) **157**   (f) **134**

7. (a) **127**   (b) **153**   (c) **194**
    (d) **155**   (e) **184**   (f) **197**

8. **336**

9. (a) **355**   (b) **406**   (c) **751**
    (d) **202**   (e) **561**   (f) **397**

Material: Four sets of **number cards** 0-9, a **die** labeled with 99, 98, and 97 twice.

Procedure: Players draw three number cards, arrange them into a 3-digit number, and throw the die. They add the number formed with the cards to the number on the die. The player with the greatest total gets all the cards that have been turned over. Play continues until all the cards are turned over. The player with the most cards wins.

 You may want to extend the lesson to include numbers close to a multiple of ten. For example, 34 + 49 can be found by adding 50 and subtracting 1.

You may also want to extend the lesson to include numbers close to a multiple of a hundred. For example, 344 + 398 can be found by adding 400 and subtracting 2.

Mental Math 8 and 9 can be used for extra practice now or later.

Workbook Exercises 6-7

Part 3 – Methods for Mental Subtraction

 Mental math strategies are reviewed here, and new ones are introduced. Your student may already be using some of the new strategies.

The following strategies will be reviewed or taught here. The illustrations are included here to help make the strategies clearer to you as the teacher — your student is not going to be drawing these illustrations.

➢ Subtract 1, 2, or 3 by counting back.
  51 – 2 = 49; count back 50, 49.
  302 – 3 = 299; count back 301, 300, 299

➢ Subtract a 1-digit number from a 2-digit or 3-digit number without renaming by subtracting ones from ones.
  155 – 4 = 151

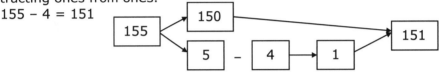

➢ Subtract 10, 20, or 30 by counting back.
  228 – 30 = 198; count back 218, 208, 198 (or count back tens first and then add ones: 21, 20, 19 tens, 198.

➢ Subtract tens from each other without renaming.
  150 – 30 = 120

➢ Subtract tens from a 2-digit or 3-digit number without renaming by subtracting from the tens.
  155 – 40 = 115

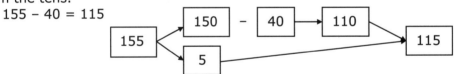

➢ Subtract a 1-digit number from a ten.
  430 – 7 = 423

➢ Subtract a 1-digit number from a 2-digit or 3-digit number when there are not enough ones by subtracting from a 10:
  176 – 8 = 168

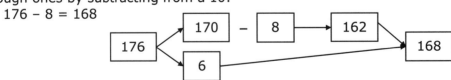

➢ Subtract a 1-digit number from a 2-digit or 3-digit number by renaming a ten as ones and recalling the subtraction fact.

$176 - 8 = 168$

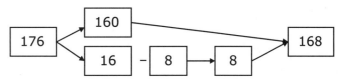

➢ Subtract tens from a 3-digit number by subtracting the tens using the same strategies as subtracting ones from a 2-digit number

$433 - 70 = 430 - 70 + 3 = 360 + 3 = 363$

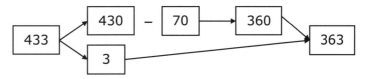

➢ Subtract hundreds from a 3-digit number by subtracting hundreds from hundreds.

$834 - 500 = 334$

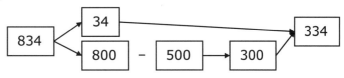

➢ Subtract a 2-digit number from a 2-digit number by subtracting first the tens and then the ones.

$75 - 38 = 37$

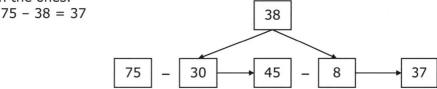

➢ Subtract a number close to 100 by first subtracting 100 and then adding back the difference.

$456 - 98 = 456 - 100 + 2 = 356 + 2 = 358$

Your student may be able to extend the strategies given in this section. Encourage your student to use mental math where possible, but allow him to fall back on the standard algorithm when he needs to.

---
(1) Subtract Ones or Tens (pp. 15-16)

- ➢ Subtract ones, tens, or hundreds from a 3-digit number when there is no renaming.
- ➢ Subtract ones or tens from a 2-digit number.

 Page 15
Illustrate the concepts on this page with actual **number discs**, base-10 blocks, or other base-10 material, if necessary. A suggested procedure is given below. In your discussion, emphasize the place value of the numbers.

Set out 6 hundreds, 5 tens, and 6 ones.

Write: 656

Ask: What number is 2 ones less than 656?

Remove 2 ones. Count back by ones. 656, 655, 654.

Write: 656 - 2 = 654

The 2 is being subtracted from the 6; they are both ones.

Ask: What number is 2 tens less than 654?

Remove 2 tens. Count back by tens. 654, 644, 634.

Write: 658 - 20 = 634

The 2 is subtracted from the 5; they are both tens.

Ask: What number is 2 hundreds less than 634?

Subtract 2 hundreds from the 6. Count back by hundreds. 634, 534, 434.

Write: 634 - 200 = 434

The 2 is being subtracted from the 6; they are both hundreds.

➤ Use **number discs** to Illustrate mental subtraction of ones from a 2-digit number when renaming occurs. Set out 5 tens and 4 ones. Tell your student you want to subtract 8. Write 54 – 8 = ? and discuss strategies to mentally find the value of 54 – 8.
- o Find the tens. Before determining the tens for the answer, look to the ones. Will subtracting 8 decrease the tens? Yes, so subtract 1 from the tens. Write 4 for the tens.

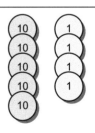

54 – 8 = ___

54 – 8 = **4_**

o   Find the ones. Discuss two methods for finding
the ones:

1. Use the subtraction fact 14 – 8 = 6 to find
the ones. You can illustrate this with the
number discs by taking one of the tens,
replacing with 10 ones, and removing 8 of
them. 6 are left.

2. Subtract from a ten and add the difference
to the ones. Show this by replacing a ten
with 2 ones, and then combining the 2 ones
with the 4 ones already there. There will be
6 ones.

Write 6 for the ones.

$$54 - 8 = 40 + 6 = 46$$

40   14

$$54 - 8 = 44 + 2 = 46$$

44   10

$$\boxed{54 - 8 = 46}$$

Write the problem 21 – 2. Tell your student that if
she is subtracting a small number such as 1, 2, or
3, they can simply count back: 20, 19.

$$21 - 2 = 19$$

Write the problem 55 – 4. Ask your student to look at
the ones. Point out that in this problem the tens will
not be increased. So the tens digit stays the same,
and we can just subtract the ones.

$$55 - 4 = 51$$

Illustrate mental subtraction of tens from a 2-digit
number. Set out 4 tens and 5 ones. Write 45 – 20 = ?
Point out that since we are subtracting tens, we can
simply subtract from tens to get the tens, and the
ones in the answer stays the same. When
subtracting smaller tens (10, 20, 30) we can also
count back by tens

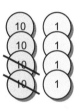

$$91 - 20 = 71$$

 Learning Task 1, p. 16

1. (a) **36**   (b) **18**   (c) **61**
    (d) **20**   (e) **50**   (f) **40**
    (g) **21**   (h) **58**   (i) **45**

 You can use Mental Math 10 for more practice.

 Workbook Exercise 8

(2) Subtract Ones, Tens, or Hundreds (pp. 16)

 ➢ Subtract ones, tens, or hundreds from a 3-digit number.

➤ Use **number discs** to illustrate mental subtraction of ones from a 3-digit number where there is renaming. Set out 3 hundreds, 5 tens, and 2 ones (or similar number). Write the equation 352 – 7 = ? and discuss strategies to find the answer.

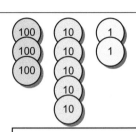

- o Find the hundreds. Since we are not subtracting tens, the hundreds will stay the same. Write 3 for the hundreds.
- o Subtract 52 – 7 using the same strategies already discussed. Write down the answer, 45. You can draw a number bond to illustrate the process.

352 – 7 = **3**__

352 – 7 = **345**

352 – 7 = 300 + 52 – 7 = 345

300   52

➤ Illustrate mental subtraction of tens from a 3-digit number where there is renaming. Set out 3 hundreds, 5 tens, and 6 ones. Write the equation 356 – 80 = ?.

356 – 80 = ___

- o Since we are not subtracting ones, we can first think of just subtracting tens. 350 tens – 8 tens can be solved using the same strategies for 35 – 8. Ask students for the answer. 35 – 8 = 27, so 35 tens – 8 tens = 27 tens. Write 25 for the tens (2 hundreds and 5 tens).
- o Find the ones. They are simply the ones we started with. Write 6 for the ones.

356 – 80 = **27**_

356 – 80 = 27**6**

356 – 80 = 350 – 80 + 6 = 276

6   350

Write a problem such as 326 – 30 = ?. Explain that with smaller tens we can count down by tens: 31 tens, 30 tens, 29 tens, the answer is 296

326 – 30 = 296

 Learning Task 2, p. 16

2.   (a) **223**   (b) **197**   (c) **403**   (d) **720**   (e) **380**   (f) **460**
     (g) **300**   (h) **300**   (i) **600**   (j) **342**   (k) **353**   (l) **608**

➤ Use Mental Math 11 and 12 for more practice.

📖 **Workbook Exercise 9**

(3) Subtract 2-Digit Numbers (p. 16)

 ➢ Subtract 2-digit numbers mentally.

 Use number discs to illustrate mental subtraction of 2-digit numbers. Write 83 – 25 = ? and display a corresponding set of 83 number discs.
- o Have your student first subtract the tens mentally and give the intermediate sum. Remove two 10-discs. 83 – 20 = 63.
- o Have your student then subtract the ones and give the final sum. Replace a 10-disc with ten 1-discs. 63 – 5 = 81.

$$83 - 25 = ?$$

$$83 \xrightarrow{-20} 63 \xrightarrow{-5} 58$$

$$83 - 25 = 58$$

 Learning Tasks 3-4, p. 16

3. **31**

4. (a) **41**   (b) **71**   (c) **30**
   (d) **11**   (e) **23**   (f) **20**

 You can use Mental Math 13 for more practice.

 Material: A hundred chart, counters or coins for each player, four sets of number cards from 0-9 and four extra 0 cards.

Procedure: Shuffle the cards and set them face down. Players take turns drawing 4 cards and arranging them into two numbers less than 100. If a 0 is drawn, it can be used as a ten to make a 1-digit number; otherwise both numbers are 2-digit numbers. For example, 3, 6, 4, and 0 are drawn. The numbers could be 40 and 36, 60 and 34, 63 and 4, etc. The player subtracts the smaller number from the larger and covers up the answer on his hundred chart with a counter or coin. The first player to get 3 in a row on the chart wins.

 Workbook Exercise 10

(4) Subtract 98 or 99 I (p. 17)

 ➢ Subtract 98 or 99 from a hundred.

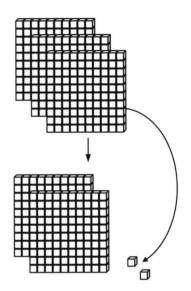

Use base-10 blocks. Set out four 100-flats. Write 300 – 98 = ? on the board. Ask your student how she can use the idea of subtracting from 100 to mentally subtract these two numbers. She can subtract 98 from one of the hundreds, leaving 2 ones.

Remove one of the hundreds and replace it with 2 ones. So the answer is one less hundred plus 2, or 202.

Point out that we can get the answer by counting back 100 and then forward 2. If we just subtract 100, we have subtracted 2 too many, so we need to add it back in.

Repeat with 400 – 99. This time, we subtract 100 and add 1.

300 – 98 = 200 + 2 = 202

You may also want to discuss subtraction of 97, 96, and 95 from hundreds.

 Learning Tasks 5-6, p. 17

5. **201**

6. (a) **101**   (b) **301**   (c) **801**
    (d) **602**   (e) **402**   (f) **702**

 Workbook Exercise 11

(5) Subtract 98 or 99 II (p. 17)

 ➢ Subtract 98 or 99 from a 3-Digit Number.

 Use base-10 blocks to illustrate subtraction of 98 from a 3-digit number. Write 423 – 98 = ? on the board and set out the corresponding number of hundreds, tens, and ones.

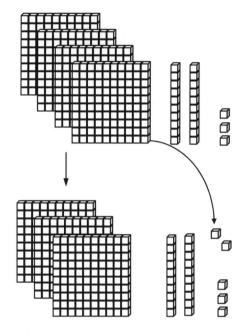

Ask your student what would happen if we subtract the 98 from one of the hundreds. The hundreds will decrease from 4 hundreds to 3 hundreds, but leave 2 ones that are not removed.

So we can find the answer by subtracting 100 and then adding 2. 423 – 100 + 2 = 325

We can count back one hundred and then forward 2.

423 – 98 = 423 – 100 + 2 = 323 + 2 = 325

 Learning Tasks 7-9, p. 17

7. **105**

8. (a) **3**   (b) **209**   (c) **506**

   (d) **206**   (e) **303**   (f) **608**

9. (a) **141**   (b) **247**   (c) **613**
   (d) **223**   (e) **456**   (f) **832**

Material: Four sets of **number cards** 0-9, a **die** labeled with 99, 98, and 97 twice.

Procedure: Players draw three number cards, arrange them into a 3-digit number, and throw the die. They subtract the number formed with the cards to the number on the die. The player with the smallest total gets all the cards that have been turned over. Play continues until all the cards are turned over. The player with the most cards wins.

➤ You may want to extend the lesson to subtracting a number close to a multiple of 100. For example, 648 – 398 can be found by subtracting 400 and then adding 2.

➤ You can use Mental Math 14 for more practice.

 Workbook Exercise 12

(6) Practice (p. 18)

➢ Practice mental math.
➢ Solve word problems involving addition and subtraction.

Use textbook Practice 1B review mental math strategies and to provide practice with word problems.

Your student should be able to determine whether to use mental math strategies or to use the addition or subtraction algorithm. Do not require that your student use mental math for all the problems. Note that mental techniques have not specifically been taught for problems 7 and 10 in Practice 1B. You may, however, want to discuss how these could be solved mentally.

For the word problems, if your student has problems, ask her to determine whether two parts are given and the whole must be found, or whether the whole and one part are given and a missing part must be found. Answers are at the back of this guide.

 Practice 1B, p. 18

1. (a) **242**   (b) **445**   (c) **905**

2. (a) **89**   (b) **161**   (c) **402**

3. (a) **98**   (b) **212**   (c) **340**

4. (a) **41**   (b) **42**   (c) **62**

5. (a) **226**   (b) **308**   (c) **501**

6.   92 – 57 = 35
     There are **35** girls.

total student: 92	
boys: 57	girls: ?

7.   185 + 28 = 213
     He made **213** sticks.

chicken satay: 185	28
US› beef, **3d›** mutton satay: ?	

8. $500 - $98 = $402
     It costs **$402**.

total money: $500	
washing machine: ?	money left: $98

9. $64 - $15 = $49
     The kettle costs **$49**.

rice cooker: $64	
kettle: ?	$15

10. (a) 215 + 285 = 500
         He sold **500** copies.

sold Saturday: 215	sold Sunday: 285
total: ?	

     (b) 285 – 215 = 70
         He sold **70** more on Sunday.

sold Sunday: 285	
sold Saturday: 215	?

(7) Practice (p. 19)

➢ Practice mental math.
➢ Solve word problems involving addition and subtraction.

Mental techniques have not specifically been taught for problems 1(c), 2(a), 2(b), 2(c), 3(b), 4(c), 5(a), 5(b), 8, or 10(a) in Practice 1C. You may, however, want to discuss how these could be solved mentally.

Practice 1C, p. 19

1. (a) **386**   (b) **327**   (c) **210**

2. (a) **250**   (b) **411**   (c) **500**

3. (a) **507**   (b) **230**   (c) **498**

4. (a) **731**   (b) **455**   (c) **178**

5. (a) **202**   (b) **359**   (c) **502**

6. (a) **304**   (b) **399**

7. Number she had at first = number she used for cake + number she had left = 255 + 45 = **300**

8. David's height = John's height + difference in height
        = 135 cm + 29 cm = **164 cm**

9. (a) Total children = number of boys + number of girls
            = 98 + 86 = **184**
    (b) Number of adults = number of children – 40
            = 184 – 40 = **144**

10. (a) Total kg sold = kg sold of first day + kg sold on second day
            = 86 kg + 54 kg = **140 kg**
    (b) kg left = kg he started with – kg he sold
            = 200 kg – 140 kg = **60 kg**

 Mental Math 15, 16, and 17 can be used for more practice.

Review

  ➢ Review all topics learned so far in *Primary Mathematics*.

▶ **Enrichment – Magic Squares**

A magic square is an array of numbers that is arranged such that
1. There are the same number of rows and columns.
2. No number is used more than once.
3. The sum of every row, column, and each of the two diagonals is the same number, called the magic sum.
4. The basic magic square is formed using consecutive numbers beginning with the number 1, but squares can be adapted by changing the order of the numbers, by adding a constant to all numbers, or by using multiples of the basic number sequence.

The first magic square was found on a scroll called Loh-Shu that was created in China around 2,800 B.C. Magic squares since spread to India, Japan, the Middle East, Africa, Europe, and America. They have been used for fortune telling, to ward off bad luck, to develop horoscopes, as protection against the plague, and have been imprinted on pieces of metal and worn as talismans. Somehow, the beauty of the math makes them seem magical.

Your student may want to try filling in magic squares.

Here are some magic squares that have been started. Have your student complete each one by placing the numbers 1 through 9 in the squares so that the sum of the rows and columns is 15.

8		6
	5	7
4	9	

4		2
	5	
	1	

Have your student find some other arrangement for the numbers 1 through 9 such that the magic sum is 15.

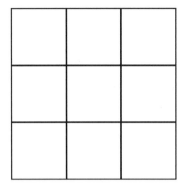 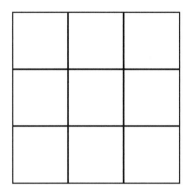

Have your student take one of the magic squares, and add 6 to each number. Ask him if he gets a magic square. What happens if he and multiplies each number by 3. Is the result a magic square? Here is the second one started:

Here is a 4 x 4 magic square that has been started. Have your student place the numbers 1 through 16 in this magic square so that the rows, columns, and two diagonals add up to 34. Have her try to find another arrangement using the same numbers that will give the same sum.

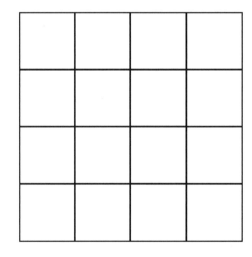

	6		16
2			5
		8	
	12		

 Workbook Review 1

Unit 2 – Multiplication and Division

In *Primary Mathematics 2A*, students learned the multiplication and division facts for 2 and 3. They should be familiar with these facts. Incorporate review of these facts with the new facts that will be learned in this unit.

Both multiplication and division are associated with the part-whole concept.

Given the number of equal parts and the number in each part, we multiply to find the whole (total).

Two related equations can be written for each multiplication situation.

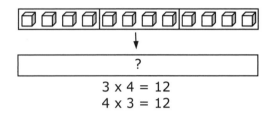

$$3 \times 4 = 12$$
$$4 \times 3 = 12$$

There are two division situations, sharing and grouping.

Sharing:
A total number (the whole) is shared into a given number of groups (parts). Divide the total by the number of parts to find the number in each part.

Grouping:
A total number (the whole) is grouped into equal parts. Divide the total by the number that goes into each part to find the number of parts.

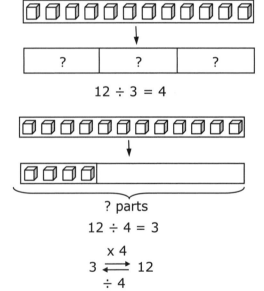

$$12 \div 3 = 4$$

? parts
$$12 \div 4 = 3$$

$$3 \overset{\times 4}{\underset{\div 4}{\rightleftarrows}} 12$$

Multiplication and division are related. The answer to $12 \div 4$ can be found by thinking of the number times 4 that equals 12.

Your student will be learning the facts for multiplication and division by 4, 5, and 10 in this unit. She will start by building the multiplication tables of 4 based on the idea of "4 more than." If she knows one fact for multiplication, she can find the next one as 4 more. She will use the multiplication facts for 4 to learn the division facts.

Review multiplication and division facts regularly, either with multiplication and division cards, worksheets, or games.

Part 1 – Multiplying and Dividing by 4

(1) Counting by Fours (pp. 20-21)

➢ Count by fours.
➢ Write multiplication equations for fours.

 Page 20

There are four stickers in each row. They can be counted by counting each row at a time. You can expand on this page as follows.

▶ Use **multilink cubes** or **connect-a-cubes** or other objects joined in fours and teach your student to count them by fours to 40.

▶ Use a **hundred chart** and have your student cover up the multiples of 4 through 40. Then have her supply the covered numbers. Repeat until she can do it fairly quickly, both forward and backward.

Practice counting by fours both forwards and backwards without the chart. Continue practicing during later lessons until he can do it easily. Let your student hold up a finger for each four, first on one hand, then the next. Until he has the facts memorized, he can count by fours until he gets to the correct number of fingers. For example, for 4 x 7 he counts by fours until he has all five fingers of one hand and two of the other up.

▶ Set out six groups of 4. Write two equations
to show the total amount.
      4 + 4 + 4 + 4 + 4 + 4 = 24.
      4 x 6 = 24.
There are 6 equal groups of 4.

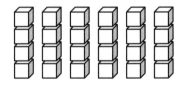

 Page 21
Learning Task 1, p. 21

(a) **12, 12**   (b) **28, 28**

1. (a) **16**   (b) **36**

 Workbook Exercise 13

(2) Related Facts (pp. 22-23)

- ➤ Relate the associated facts 4 x _____ and _____ x 4.
- ➤ Build the multiplication table for 4
- ➤ Use related facts to find unknown facts.

 Put sets of 4 (**multilink cubes or legos**) in a rectangular array. Show that the array can be divided into either rows or columns, and that the array can be represented by:
4 + 4 + 4 + 4 + 4 = 4 x 5
5 + 5 + 5 + 5 = 5 x 4
Point out that if she knows 4 x 5, then she also knows 5 x 4.

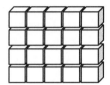

 Learning Tasks 2-3, p. 22

2. **32**

3. **20**; **28, 28**; **36, 36**

 Learning Tasks 4-5, pp. 22-23
As your student does learning task 4, point out that each fact is 4 more than the one before it, and 4 less than the one after it. If she knows one fact, she can find the one "above" it or "below" it by adding 4 or subtracting 4, as shown in learning task 5.

4. **12, 16, 20, 24, 28, 32, 36, 40**
   8, 12, 16, 20, 24, 28, 32, 36, 40

5. **24**

 Set out a pattern of blocks like that shown here. Write

        2 x 3 = 6   4 x 3 = 12

Ask him if he sees a relationship between the two equations. Four times a number is double 2 times a number. Tell him he can use doubling and his multiplication facts of 2 to figure out the multiplication facts of 4 by doubling the double. For example, to find 4 x 4, double 4 is 8, double 8 is 16. 4, 8, 16.

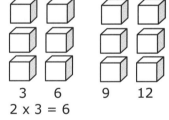

3   6   9   12
2 x 3 = 6
4 x 3 = 2 x 6 = 12

 Have your student do Mental Math 18.

 Workbook Exercises 14-15

(3) Word Problems

> ➢ Solve word problems involving multiplication by 4
> ➢ Memorize multiplication facts for 4

➤ Discuss some word problems with your student. He should determine what the problem wants him to find and what information is given. He should be able to tell you whether there are equal groups, how many equal groups, and how much is in each group. Have him write an equation for each problem. Allow him to act out the problem with connect-a-cubes or other objects they can put into groups or make drawings, if necessary.

- o Jeremy bought 4 books. Each book cost $6. How much did he pay for the books? (4 x $6 = $24)

- o A plastic bag can hold 4 apples. How many apples can 7 plastic bags hold? (4 x 7 = 28)

- o Marisol wants to wrap 6 presents. Each present needs 4 feet of ribbon. How many total feet of ribbon does she need to wrap all 6 presents?   (6 x 4 ft= 24 ft)

- o There are 8 rows of desks in a classroom. There are 4 desks in each row. There are 35 students. Are there enough desks for each student?   (8 x 4 = 32. No)

- o There are 4 monkeys in a zoo. Each monkey eats 3 bananas in the morning and 4 bananas in the afternoon.
  a) How many bananas do they eat in the morning? (4 x 3 = 12)
  b) How many bananas do they eat in the afternoon? (4 x 4 = 16)
  c) How many bananas do they eat altogether? (12 + 16 = 28 or 4 x 7 = 28)

➤ Help your student memorize the facts for 4. The following activities could be used. They can be continued as you proceed to other units.

Have your say or "chant" the multiplication facts periodically during the next few lessons - "four times one is four, four times two is eight, four times three is twelve …", or "four one four, four two eight, four three twelve… " first with his list of multiplication sentences to see, and then without them.

Have your student to Mental Math worksheets 19-20

Make a set of **fact cards** for the multiplication facts of 4. Shuffle and show your student each card. If he gives the correct answer, put it in his pile; if not, tell him the correct answer and put it in your pile. Repeat with your pile until he has all the cards. If your student can handle timed drills, show him the card for a certain number of seconds (which you count silently). If he gets the answer correct within the time limit, he gets the card; if not, tell him the answer and keep the card. Repeat until he has all the cards. In subsequent practices, reduce the time limit. Mix in some of the multiplication facts for 2 and 3 he is having trouble with.

Use or four sets of **number cards** 1-10. Shuffle and place face down. The student turns over the cards one at a time and supplies the fact for 4 times the number drawn. If correct, he places the cards in one pile; if wrong, he places them in a second pile. Repeat with the second pile.

Make a game board with multiples of 4 in random order. Make two sets of number cards 1-9 which fit into the spaces. Shuffle the cards and place them face down. The student draws one card at a time and lays the card on the multiple of 4. For example, she draws a 9. She

4	32	8	12	4
28	20	8	24	12
16	28	32	40	20
40	24	36	16	36

puts it on one of the 36 squares. You can time her and let her see if she can beat her previous time. She can also see how soon she gets 3 or 4 in a row.

Play Concentration. Write the following on **index cards**: 4 x 1, 4 x 2, 4 x 3, 4 x 4, 4 x 5, 4 x 6, 4 x 7, 4 x 8, 4 x 9, 4 x 10. Write the answers on another set of cards: 4, 8, 12, 16, 20, 24, 28, 32, 36, 40. Mix them up and lay them face down in a 5 x 4 array. Your student turns up two at a time. If they match, he removes them. If not, he turns them face down. Repeat with another two. Continue until all have been removed.

Play War. Use **playing cards** (with face cards removed) and a **dice** with the 5 and 6 covered up with tape and replaced with 3 and 4. Shuffle the cards and deal the deck to all the players. Each player draws a card from his cards and throws the dice. His score is the product of the number on the dice and the card. The player with the highest product gets all the cards. Game continues until one player has all the cards.

 Workbook Exercise 16-17

(4) Division by 4 (pp. 23-24)

 ➢   Relate division by 4 to multiplication by 4.

➤ Use small objects, such as **counters**, to demonstrate the relationship between division by 4 and multiplication by 4. Set out 24 counters and 4 paper plates or bows, or draw 4 circles, and tell your student that we want to divide 24 objects into 4 equal groups. Tell her that the total (point to it) divided by the number of equal groups (point to the circles) gives the number in each group.

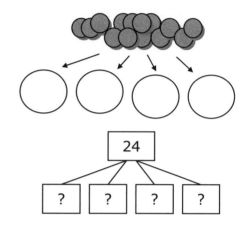

Draw a number bond with 4 parts with a question mark in each part. Point out that 24 is the total, and there are four equal parts.

Before letting your student divide up the counters, remind him that the number in each group times the number of equal groups gives the total. If he can think of what number times 4 gives a total of 24 they will know how many are in each group. Ask for the answer to 6 x ___ = 24. If 6 x 4 = 24, then 24 ÷ 4 = 6. Write the equations and draw an arrow diagram to show the relationship between multiplication and division.

$$24 \div 4 = 6$$
$$6 \times 4 = 24$$

$$6 \underset{\div 4}{\overset{\times 4}{\rightleftharpoons}} 24$$

Put the counters back together and tell your student that we now want to divide the counters into groups of 4. Point out that we still have a total amount, but now we are grouping by 4 and want to find the number of equal groups, or parts. Ask how many will go into each group. To answer this, they can still use the multiplication facts to think of the number times 4 which gives a total of 24.

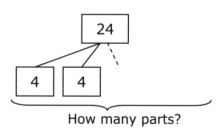

How many parts?

Arrange the counters in an array and have your student write two multiplication equations and 2 division equations.

$4 \times 6 = 24 \quad 24 \div 4 = 6$
$6 \times 4 = 24 \quad 24 \div 6 = 4$

 Write the following problems, one pair at a time, first the multiplication problem, followed by the corresponding division problem, and have your student supply the missing number.

___ x 4 = 4	4 ÷ 4 = ___
___ x 4 = 8	8 ÷ 4 = ___
___ x 4 = 12	12 ÷ 4 = ___
___ x 4 = 16	16 ÷ 4 = ___
___ x 4 = 20	20 ÷ 4 = ___
___ x 4 = 24	24 ÷ 4 = ___
___ x 4 = 28	28 ÷ 4 = ___
___ x 4 = 32	32 ÷ 4 = ___
___ x 4 = 36	36 ÷ 4 = ___
___ x 4 = 40	40 ÷ 4 = ___

 Learning Tasks 6-8, pp. 23-24
6(a) illustrates sharing; 6(b) illustrates grouping.

6. (a) **3, 3**   (b) **3, 3, 3**

7. **2   5, 5   8   7, 7**

8. (a) **1**   (b) **4**   (c) **8**
    (d) **6**   (e) **3**   (f) **10**

Workbook Exercise 18, #1-2

(5) Division Facts

 ➤ Start memorizing division facts for 4.

➤ By now, your student should begin to recognize whether a given number is a multiple of 2, 3, or 4 up to ten times.

Use number cards with the numbers 2, 3, 4, 6, 8, 9, 10, 12, 14, 15, 16, 18, 20, 21, 22, 24, 27, 28, 30, 32, 36, 40. Shuffle. Draw one at a time and ask your student to supply as many multiplication facts she can for each.

➤ Help your student memorize the division facts for 4, using fact cards, games, or other methods, such as adaptations of the activities given for multiplication, or the following games.

 Material: A **game board** with the numbers 1 through 10. (You can make the game board as large as you want. You can use the back of a laminated hundred chart. Write the numbers 1-10 randomly in the squares using dry-erase or wet-erase markers.) A set of division cards for the division facts for 2, 3, and 4. (Use index cards and write the division expressions on them: 40 ÷ 4, 36 ÷ 4, ... , 30 ÷ 3, etc.) **Counters** of different colors for each player. You can use pennies and dimes for 2 players.

Procedure: Shuffle the cards and place them face down. Players take turns drawing a card and placing a marker on the board for the answer. The winner is the first to get three markers in a row.

Material: A 5 x 5 **game board** with the numbers 2, 3, 4, 6, 8, 9, 10, 12, 12, 14, 15, 16, 16, 18, 20, 21, 22, 24, 24, 27, 28, 30, 32, 36, 40 randomly placed. (You can use the back of a hundred board and write the numbers in the squares. For a larger game board, use all 100 squares and repeat the numbers.) A dice with the 1, 5 and 6 covered up with a sticker and replaced with 2, 3, and 4. **Counters** of different colors for each player, or coins.

Procedure: The players take turns throwing the dice and placing a marker on a number that would be 1 times, 2 times, 3 times, or 4 times the number thrown. The winner is the first to get three markers in a row. Your student may notice that 28 can count as a multiple of 2, or 36 as a multiple of 3.

➤ Use Mental Math 21 for more practice.

(6) Word Problems (p. 24)

> Solve word problems involving division by 4.
> Solve word problems involving multiplication or division by 2, 3, or 4.

Learning Task 9, p. 24
Discuss these problems in terms of whole and equal parts. You can let your student act out the problems with objects. You can draw a diagram, either a number bond, a drawing, or bars illustrating the problem. Do not require your student to draw bar diagrams yet.

In (a), we are given the number of groups (4 days) and asked to find how much goes into each group (how much she saved each day.
In (b), we are given the number that goes in each group, and asked to find the number of groups. In both situations, we need to divide.

9.   (a)

total money: $32			
day 1 ?	day 2 ?	day 3 ?	day 4 ?

Amount saved each day   = total money ÷ number of days
= 32 ÷ 4
= **8**

(b)

total money: $40			
day 1 $4	day 2 $4	. . .	day ? $4

Number of days = total money ÷ amount each day
= 40 ÷ 4 = 10
= **10**

You may want to discuss some additional problems. Let your student act out the problems using objects or drawing pictures to solve them. Write equations for each problem. Use the following or the problems in Practice 2A. These problems involve mutliplication and division. Help your student determine which operation is needed by determining whether a whole is given or not. Solutions to the practice are given in the back of this guide.

Encourage your student to write the measurement units with the answers, not just the numerical answer (e.g., $, m, kg, in. ...)

> A box of 4 toy cars cost $9. Josh bought 12 cars.
>   a) How many boxes did he buy? (12 ÷ 4 = 3)
>   b) How much did he pay? (3 x $9 = $27)

➤ You have 24 toothpicks.
  a) How many equal sized squares can you form with the toothpicks? (6 with sides one toothpick long, or 3 with sides two toothpicks long)
  b) How many equal sized triangles of equal sides can you form with the toothpicks? (8 with sides 1 toothpick long, 4 with sides 2 toothpicks long)

➤ A cook makes 24 cookies and 20 brownies. Somebody ate 4 cookies and 5 brownies while they were cooling. The cook put 4 cookies and 3 brownies on each plate. How many plates did she use?
Total cookies = 24 – 4 = 20
Total brownies = 20 – 5 = 15
Number of plates = 20 ÷ 4 = 5 or 15 ÷ 3 = 5 (show how the number of plates is the same for both)

 Workbook Exercise 18 #3-5

(7) Practice (p. 25)

➤ Solve word problems involving multiplication or division by 2, 3, or 4.

Practice 2A, p. 25

1. (a) **12**   (b) **28**   (c) **8**

2. (a) **1**   (b) **8**   (c) **4**

3. (a) **24**   (b) **40**   (c) **32**

4. (a) **2**   (b) **5**   (c) **10**

5. (a) **9**   (b) **3**   (c) **6**

6. Total = number in each part x number of parts
   Total passengers = number of passengers in a taxi x number of taxis
   = 4 x 5 = **20**

7. amount in each part = total ÷ number of parts
   amount in each bag = total amount ÷ number of bags
   = 16 kg ÷ 4 = **4 kg**

8. Total = number of parts x number in each part
   Total books borrowed = number of children x number of books for each child
   = 6 x 4 = **24**

9. cost of one part = total ÷ number of parts
   cost of one T-shirt = total cost ÷ number of T-shirts
   = $40 ÷ 4 = **$10**

10. Total = number of parts x amount in each part
    Total length = number of covers x length for each cover
    = 4 x 8 m = **32 m**

11. number in each part = total ÷ number of parts
    number of glasses in each box = total glasses ÷ number of boxes
    = 36 ÷ 4 = **9**

Part 2 – Multiplying and Dividing by 5

---

(1) Counting by Fives (pp. 26-28)

- ➤ Count by fives.
- ➤ Write multiplication equations for fives.

 Page 26

Discuss this page. The picture cards are being counted in groups of 5.

 Use a **hundred chart** and have your student cover up the multiples of 5 through 50. Have your student supply the covered numbers. Repeat until he can do it fairly quickly, both forward and backward.

Practice counting by fives both forward and backward without the chart. Continue practicing during later lessons until he can do it easily. Let your student hold up a finger for each five.

Write: 5   10   15   20   25   30   35   40   45   50
Or have yours student color in the fives on a hundred chart.
Ask him if he sees a pattern. Each number ends in a five or a zero.

Give your student a pile of nickels and have her count the amount of money by counting by fives.

Use Mental Math 22 for more practice.

 Learning Tasks 1-3, pp. 27-28

1. (a) **15, 15**   (b) **40, 40**

2. **45**

3. (a) **30¢**   (b) **$35**

 Workbook Exercise 19

(2) Multiplication Facts (p. 28)

- ➢ Memorize multiplication facts for fives.
- ➢ Solve word problems involving multiplication by 5

➤ Give your student **linking cubes** linked in fives or the 5-unit bars. Ask her to set out the number of bars that would give a total of 30 and to write two multiplication equations for the array.

Ask your student how many more cubes are needed to show 5 x 7. 5 x 7 is 5 more than 5 x 6. Have him add another 5-unit to the displayed bars. Point out that he can use the multiplication fact 5 x 6 = 30 to find 5 x 7 = 35 by adding 5 to the product of 5 and 6.

Ask your student to write two multiplication equations for this array.

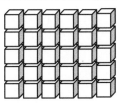

5 x 6 = 30
6 x 5 = 30

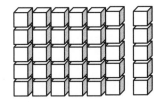

5 x 7 = 30 + 5 = 35

5 x 7 = 35

7 x 5 = 35

➤ You may want to teach your student that one way to multiply by 5 is to take half the ten of the number you are multiplying by 5.
For example:
    4 x 5   The ten is 40, and half the ten is 20.
    7 x 5   The ten is 70, and half the ten is 35.

➤ Use Mental Math 23-24 for more practice.

 Learning Tasks 4-5, p. 28

4. **20**   **45, 45**

5. (a) **35**   (b) **30**   (c) **5**
    (d) **25**   (e) **10**   (f) **50**

➤ Discuss the following word problems.

- ➢ Melanie bought 5 dolls. Each doll cost $6. How much did she pay for the dolls? (5 x $6 = $30)
- ➢ A box can hold 8 cupcakes. How many cupcakes can 5 such boxes hold? (5 x 8 = 40)

➤ Cecily wants to sew 9 pillow cases. For each pillow case she needs 5 feet of
   material. How many feet of material does she need? (5 ft x 9 = 45 ft)
➤ There are 7 elephants in a zoo. Each elephant eats 5 bundles of hay in the
   morning and 4 bundles in the afternoon.
   a) How many bundles of hay do they eat in the morning? (5 x 7 = 35)
   b) How many bundles of hay do they eat in the afternoon? (4 x 7 = 28)
   c) How many more bundles do they eat in the morning than in the
       afternoon? (35 – 28 = 7)

➤ Help your student memorize the multiplication facts for 5. They are likely to be
   easy to remember. You can use the activities similar to those given for
   memorizing the facts for 4. Include earlier facts your student may be having
   difficulty with. If playing war with cards and dice, cover up the 6 and 1 on the
   dice and replace them with 4 and 5.

Workbook Exercise 20

(3) Division by 5 (p. 28)

➢ Relate division by 5 to multiplication by 5.
➢ Solve word problems involving division by 5.

➤ Remind your student that multiplication and division are related, and that to find a number divided by 5, such as 35 ÷ 5, they can think of the number times 5 that gives 35. If necessary, do activities similar to those given for division by 4.

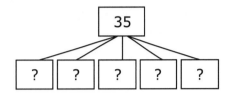

 Learning Tasks 6-7, p. 28

6.	**3**		**8, 8**			
7.	(a) **6**	(b) **1**	(c) **5**
	(d) **2**	(e) **10**	(f) **9**

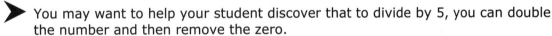

➤ Continue to work with your student on memorizing the mutliplication and division facts for 2, 3, 4, and 5. Use Mental Math 25 for more practice.

Your student should also be able to recognize that a number is part of the 2, 3, 4, or 5 pattern.

➤ You may want to help your student discover that to divide by 5, you can double the number and then remove the zero.
    20 ÷ 5   Double 20 is 40. Remove the zero to get 4.
    45 ÷ 5   Double 45 is 90. Remove the zero to get 9.

Workbook Exercise 21

(4) Word Problems (p. 29)

  ➢ Solve word problems involving multiplication or division by 2, 3, 4, or 5.

➤ Discuss some of the word problems in Practice 2B, or the following problems. Your student can act out the problems with objects or use diagrams to solve, if necessary. She should determine first whether a total is given or needs to be found. If it is given, it is either a subtraction or division problem. For a division problem, she needs to see that the problems gives a total amount and either the number of equal groups and asks for the number that goes into each group, or the problem are gives the number that goes into each group and asks for the number of groups. If a total needs to be found, it is either an addition or multiplication problem. For a multiplication problem, she needs to see that the problem gives the number of equal groups and the number that goes into each group and asks for the total.

➢ A box of 25 cookies was shared among 5 children equally. How many cookies did each child get? ($25 \div 5 = 5$)

➢ A box of 40 cookies was shared among 5 boys.

    a) How many cookies did each boy get? ($40 \div 5 = 8$)

    b) How many cookies altogether did 4 of the boys get? ($8 \times 4 = 32$)

    c) If 5 of the cookies were dropped and could not be eaten, how many cookies would each of the 5 boys get? ($35 \div 5 = 7$)

    d) If one boy decided he did not want any of the 40 cookies, how many cookies would the rest of the boys get if they all got an equal number? ($40 \div 4 = 10$)

➢ On a test, 5 points were given for each correct answer and 3 points subtracted for each wrong answer. The test had 10 questions. Maria got 8 correct answers.

    a) How many points did she get for correct answers? ($5 \times 8 = 40$)

    b) How many points were subtracted for wrong answers? ($2 \times 3 = 6$)

    c) What was her final score? ($40 - 6 = 34$)

Practice 2B, p. 29

1. (a) **25**   (b) **20**   (c) **35**

2. (a) **3**   (b) **5**   (c) **1**

3. (a) **5**   (b) **45**   (c) **15**

4. (a) **4**   (b) **6**   (c) **9**

5. (a) **8**   (b) **10**   (c) **7**

6. 1 kg of prawns costs $8
   5 kg of prawns cost $8 x 5 = **$40**

7. 1 cake costs $7
   5 cakes cost $7 x 5 = **$35**

8. 5 people spent $45
   1 person spent $45 ÷ 5 = **$9**

9. 5 items are in 1 packet.
   25 items are in 25 ÷ 5 = **5** packets

9. 1 kg cost $5
   3 kg cost $5 x 3 = **$15**

10. 5 kg cost $30
    1 kg cost $30 ÷ 5 = **$6**

Part 3 – Multiplying and Dividing by 10

(1) Multiplication by 10 (pp. 30-31)

➢ Count by tens.
➢ Learn multiplication facts for ten.

 Your student should already have had a lot of practice counting by 10. Here she or he will associate counting by tens with multiplication.

Write:
         10 x 1 = 10
         10 x 2 = 20
         10 x 3 = 30
         10 x 4 = 40
         10 x 5 = 50
         10 x 6 = 60
         10 x 7 = 70
         10 x 8 = 80
         10 x 9 = 90
         10 x 10 = 100

Ask your student if she sees a pattern. A "0" is added to the number being multiplied by 10. She knows that 6 tens = 60. 6 tens is the same as 6 x 10.

Include the multiplication facts for 10 during fact practice activities. If playing "War" with cards and a dice as described above for fours and fives, cover up the one on the dice with a sticker and replace it with a 10, and replace the 6 with a 4.

Have your student fill out the chart in Mental Math 26. Point out that out of 100 multiplication facts, she has learned all except for 16 of them.

 Learning Tasks 1-4, pp. 30-31

1. (a) **40, 40**   (b) **60, 60**

2. (a) **70¢**   (b) **$80**

3. **40, 40**   **70, 70**

4. (a) **30**   (b) **100**   (c) **90**
    (d) **20**   (e) **10**   (f) **60**

 Workbook Exercise 22

(2) Division by 10 (p. 31)

 ➢ Divide by 10.

 Write the following equations, asking your student to supply the answers.

$10 \div 10 = 1$
$20 \div 10 = 2$
$30 \div 10 = 3$
$40 \div 10 = 4$
$50 \div 10 = 5$
$60 \div 10 = 6$
$70 \div 10 = 7$
$80 \div 10 = 8$
$90 \div 10 = 9$
$100 \div 10 = 10$

Ask your student if she sees a pattern. To divide a ten by ten, he can remove a "0". Illustrate with base-10 blocks, if necessary. If he has 4 tens (40) and divides them into 4 groups, each group gets 1 ten.

 Learning Tasks 5-6, p. 31

5. **5**   **8, 8**

6. (a) **6**   (b) **3**   (c) **1**
     (d) **4**   (e) **10**   (f) **9**

 Workbook Exercise 23

(3) Practice (pp. 32-34)

➢ Practice multiplication and division by 2, 3, 4, 5, and 10.

 Use Practices 2C, 2D, and 2E and Mental Math 27 and 28 to review this unit. They can be done orally by your student or independently. You can save some of the practices for review during later units, and use the Mental Math pages over again or later. Continue to have your student practice multiplication and division facts as needed. Your student should be proficient in the facts for 2, 3, 4, 5 and 10 before *Primary Mathematics 3A*.

 Practice 2C, p. 32

1. (a) **40**   (b) **10**   (c) **70**

2. (a) **6**   (b) **2**   (c) **7**

3. (a) **60**   (b) **50**   (c) **100**

4. (a) **3**   (b) **1**   (c) **9**

5. (a) **10**   (b) **8**   (c) **5**

6. Total payment = number of tickets x cost per ticket
    = 10 x \$7 = **\$70**

7. Number of packets = total beads ÷ number of beads in each packet
    = 40 ÷ 10 = **4**

8. Total money = number of jars x cost for each jar
    = 10 x \$3 = **\$30**

9. Cost of one can = total cost ÷ number of cans
    = \$80 ÷ 10 = **\$8**

10. Total weight = 10 x 5 kg = **50 kg**

US› 11. Number of boxes = 60 ÷ 10 = **6**
3d›   Number of trays = 60 ÷ 10 = **6**

Practice 2D, p. 33

1. (a) **24**   (b) **20**   (c) **30**

2. (a) **3**   (b) **4**   (c) **4**

3. (a) **32**   (b) **25**   (c) **36**

4. (a) **8**   (b) **7**   (c) **7**

5. (a) **45**   (b) **30**   (c) **80**

6. Cost of 1 m = total cost ÷ number of meters
   = $36 ÷ 4 = **$9**

7. Total length = number of dresses x length for each dress
   = 5 x 3 m = **15 m**

8. Number of puzzles = total money ÷ cost of each puzzle
   = $50 ÷ $10 = **5**

9. Number of chairs in a row = total chairs ÷ number of rows
   = 24 ÷ 4 = **6**

10. Number of boxes = total pies ÷ number in each box
    = 40 ÷ 5 = **8**

11. Total cards = 8 x 4 = **32**

 Practice 2E, p. 34

1. (a) **12**   (b) **40**   (c) **90**

2. (a) **5**   (b) **5**   (c) **5**

3. (a) **36**   (b) **70**   (c) **16**

4. (a) **6**   (b) **8**   (c) **1**

5. (a) **100**   (b) **28**   (c) **15**

6. Number of sets = total length ÷ length for each set = 20 m ÷ 4 m = **5**

7. Number in each box = total cupcakes ÷ number of boxes = 50 ÷ 5 = **10**

US› 8. Total oranges = number of bags x number of oranges in each bag
   = 6 x 10 = **60**

3d› Total eggs = number of trays x number of eggs in each tray = 6 x 10 = **60**

10. Number of tents = total scouts ÷ number of scouts for each tent
    = 36 ÷ 4 = **9**

11. Money for each boy = total money ÷ number of boys = $16 ÷ 2 = **$8**

Review

   ➤ Review all topics

➤ Use Review A to review concepts learned so far in Primary Mathematics. You may want to do this review as a lesson, discussing your student's answers.

 Review A, p. 35

1. (a) **800**   (b) **648**   (c) **902**

2. (a) **260**   (b) **9**   (c) **401**

3. (a) **12**   (b) **30**   (c) **70**

4. (a) **10**   (b) **6**   (c) **9**

5. Number that did not turn up = total - number that turned up
    = 1,000 – 958 = **42**

6. Total sold = number sold in morning + number sold in afternoon
    =105 + 95 = **200**

7. Number of jars = total cost ÷ cost per jar = \$35 ÷ \$5 = **7**

8. (a) Number of boxes = total glasses ÷ number of glasses in a box
    = 50 ÷ 10 = **5**

    (b) Total spent = number of boxes x cost for each box = 5 x \$9 = **\$45**

9. (a) Cost of stove = cost of oven – difference = \$488 - \$85 = **\$403**

    (b) Total cost = cost of oven + cost of TV = \$488 + \$403 = **\$891**

Workbook Review 2

Unit 3 – Money

Part 1 – Dollars and Cents

(1) Dollars and Cents (pp. 36-37)

➢ Count money in a set of bills and coins.
➢ Recognize, read, and write the decimal notation for money.

Students learned to count money in a set of coins (up to $1) or bills (up to $10) in *Primary Mathematics 1B*. Here your student will learn to count money in sets of bills and coins up to $100, to convert from dollars and cents to cents and vice-versa, and to make change for $1, $5, and $10. He will also learn to write amounts of money up to $100 in words.

The concept of decimals has not yet been taught. The decimal point should be presented as a dot separating dollars from cents. Decimals will be taught in *Primary Mathematics 4B*.

3d› The U.S. term *bills* will be used for *notes* in this guide.

Use **coins**. Review counting sets of coins less than $1.

US› Discuss strategies for counting the coins, such as counting the money in quarters first, then dimes, then nickels, then pennies, or grouping a nickel with a quarter to make 30 cents. Practice counting by 25: 25, 50, 75, 100. Make sure your student knows the names of the coins (quarters, dimes, nickels, pennies) and values.

Use $1, $5, and $10 **bills**. Review counting sets of bills less than $10.

Use **coins** and **bills**. Show your student a dollar bill and a coin, such as ten cents. Ask her to tell you the amount of money (one dollar and ten cents). Ask her to write the amount down. She may write $1 10¢. Tell her she can write the amount as $1.10. The dot separates the cents from the dollars. We don't use the symbol for cents when we write it this way.

 Page 36-37

Show your student some bills only, such as two dollar bills. Ask her for the amount of money. We can write it as:

    $2   or $2.00   or   two dollars

The **.00** shows that there are no cents.

Give her two 10-cent coins and one 1-cent coin. Ask her for the amount of money. We can write it as

21¢   or $0.21   or   twenty-one cents

Ask her how many cents are in a dollar. Give her some change totaling 99¢ and have her count it. Write

$0.99

Add one more cent. Write

$1.00

Since adding a cent makes one dollar, we use two 0's as place holders after the dot to show that there are no cents. When writing money, she should always write two digits after the dot. So we write $4.30, not $4.3.

Give her a dollar and five cents. Write

$1.05

Tell her that since we always want to write two numbers after the dot when writing numbers, we write a zero first when we have less than 10 cents in coins. Point out that if we wrote $1.5 it would be the same as $1.50, or a dollar and fifty cents, rather than five cents. Tell her that $1.05 can also be written as

1 dollar and 5 cents

 Give your student some coins and bills totaling less than $10 and have him count them. Help him determine useful ways to arrange the money to simplify counting it. Larger denominations should generally be counted first. Have him write the amount down using decimal notation.

 Write an amount less than $10 down in decimal notation. Have her read the amount as dollars and cents and then give you the exact amount in coins and bills.

Learning Tasks 1-3, pp. 37-38

1. (a) **$23.30** (b) **$4.32**   (c) **$8**   (d) **$1.65**

2. Student gives the amount verbally in dollars and cents

Workbook Exercise 24

(2) Writing Money Amounts (p. 38)

  ➢ Write amounts of money in words.

 Learning Tasks 3, p. 38

3.   (a) **4** dollars, **75** cents   (b) **8** dollars, **0** cents   (c) **0** dollars, **35** cents

 Review the spelling of number words with your student.

Have your student write out task 3 using number words.
(a)   four dollars and seventy-five cents
(b)   eight dollars
(c)   thirty-five cents

Write some other amounts of money less than $10 and have your student write the words for it. Include some where the amount of cents is less than 10. $9.05 is nine dollars and five cents. You can also include amounts of money up to $1000. $483.32 is four hundred eighty-three dollars and thirty-two cents. Tell your student that the dollars are written out in words when writing a check. If you have an old check book, you can have him write the words on the checks (have him write out the cents too, though that isn't usually done on checks).

Workbook Exercises 25-26

(3) Converting Money (pp. 38-39)

 ➢ Convert money from one denomination to another.

➤ Use **coins**. Ask your student for different combinations of coins that total 10¢. Draw a chart with headings for the different coin denominations, 1¢, 5¢, 10¢, (or penny, nickel, and dime). Help him come up with a systematic way of keeping track of the different combinations. For example, he could start with all 1¢ coins, and then trade in 5 of them for 5¢ coins. Or he could start with a dime, and start breaking it down into the next smallest denomination.

1¢	5¢	10¢
10	0	0
5	1	0
0	2	0
0	0	1

Repeat with another denomination (**US›** a quarter, **3d›** twenty-cent coin).

US› The chart at the right shows different ways to make a quarter.

Try some other amounts, not too large, such as $0.31. Keep it simple and do not require all combinations if there are too many (**US›** there are 292 different possible coin combinations for making $1 from pennies, dimes, nickels, quarters, and half-dollars).

quarter	dime	nickel	penny
1			
	2	1	
	2		5
	1	3	
	1	2	5
	1	1	10
	1		15
		5	
		4	5
		3	10
		2	15
		1	20
			25

 Learning Tasks 4-7, pp. 38-39

4. (a) **100**   (b) **10**   (c) **20**

US› 5. (a) **1.50**   (b) **1.50**
3d› 5. (a) **1.50**   (b) **1.40**

US› 6. (a) **2**   (b) **4**
3d› 6. (a) **4**   (b) **10**

US› 7. **$23**
3d› 7. **$31**

Have your student find all the combinations of bills that make a given number of dollars, such as the amount in learning task 7. (**US›** For $23 there are 8 different combinations).

 Guessing game

Material: Coins and **bills**.

Procedure: Hold some coins behind your back totaling less than $1 and tell your student the total amount and number of coins. Ask him to tell you how many coins of each denomination you have. Do the same with bills, or coins and bills up to a total of $10.00. The coins should add up to less than $10. For example, you have a five-dollar bill, a 1 dollar bill, a quarter, and a dime. Tell him you have 2 bills and 2 coins and a total of $6.30. Keep the number of coins and bills small. Allow your student to work out the answer for your combination with other coins and bills.

Let your student pick out an amount of money and tell you the total amount and the number of bills and coins. You have to guess his combination mentally, without resorting to actual bills and coins.

(4) Changing Dollars and Cents (p. 39)

 ➤ Convert dollars and cents to cents, and cents to dollars and cents.

 Ask your student for the number of cents in a dollar. Give her a set of coins that total to more than $1, such as $1.25, and ask her to count it and write the amount in cents. Then ask her to trade in a dollars worth of coins for a dollar bill and write the amount in dollars and cents.

125¢ = $1.25

Do a few other examples, including amounts of coins greater than $2 or $3.

 Learning Tasks 8-9, p. 39

8. (a) **0.65**   (b) **1.65**

9. (a) **85**   (b) **120**
    (c) **200**   (d) **205**

 Workbook Exercise 27

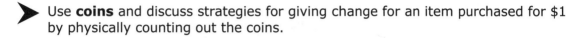

(5) Making Change for $1 (p. 40)

 ➢ Make change for $1.
➢ Subtract cents from $1.

➤ Use **coins** and discuss strategies for giving change for an item purchased for $1 by physically counting out the coins.

For example, for an item that costs $0.63
        Say "64, 65" and count out 2 pennies
        Say "75" and count out a dime
        Say "one dollar" and count out a quarter.
        The change is 2 pennies, a dime, and a quarter. 37¢.
Or
        Say "64, 65" and count out 2 pennies
        Say "70, 75, 80" and count out 3 nickels
        Say "90, one dollar" and count out 2 dimes. 37¢

Give your student coins and pretend you are buying something for less than $1 and have her give you change under different circumstances, such as when she has no 5-cent coins.

➤ Use examples to discuss with your student different ways for finding the difference between $1 and an amount of money less than $1. Since $1 is 100¢, this is a review of making 100.

Your student can count on, first by tens and then by ones, to 100. For example:
$$+\ 30¢ \qquad +\ 7¢$$
$$63¢ \longrightarrow 93¢ \longrightarrow \$1$$

$$\$1 - 63¢ = 37¢$$

Or he can find the digit that makes 9 with the tens and 10 with the ones, as learned in unit 1. ($1 - 63¢ = 9 tens and 10 ones – 6 tens and 3 ones)

 Learning Tasks 10-12, p. 40

10. **55¢**

11. (a) **40¢**   (b) **15¢**   (c) **90¢**   (d) **95¢**

12. (a) **80¢**   (b) **25¢**

 Workbook Exercise 28

(6) Making Change for $5 or $10 (p. 40)

> ➢ Make change for $5 or $10.
> ➢ Subtract from $10.

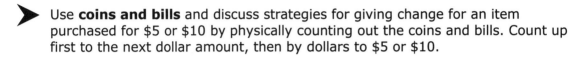

Use **coins and bills** and discuss strategies for giving change for an item purchased for $5 or $10 by physically counting out the coins and bills. Count up first to the next dollar amount, then by dollars to $5 or $10.

Give your student coins and bills and pretend you are buying something for less than $10 and have her give you change.

Use examples to show your student different ways for finding the difference between $10 and an amount of money less than $10.

She can count on to the dollar amount, and then count on to $10. For example:

$$\overset{+\ 70¢}{\$6.30 \longrightarrow \$7} \overset{+\ \$3}{\longrightarrow \$10}$$

$$\$10 - \$6.30 = \$3.70$$

Or she can think of the $10 as $9 and 100¢ and subtract the dollars from $9 and the cents from 100¢ using the mental math strategies already learned in unit 1.

$$\$10 - \$6.30$$
$$\swarrow \quad \searrow$$
$$\$9 \quad 100¢$$

$$\$9 - \$6 = \$3 \searrow$$
$$\quad \$3.70$$
$$100¢ - 30¢ = 70¢ \nearrow$$

 Learning Tasks 13-14, p. 40

13. (a) **$5.70**   (b) **$7.35**
14. (a) **$4.60**   (b) **$3.05**

 Workbook Exercise 29

(7) Word Problems (p. 41)

 ➢ Solve word problems involving money.

 Use **coins** and **bills** and the **store cards** (see description in the suggested manipulatives in the preface), or items from around the house labeled with amounts less than $10 in decimal notation and less than $1. Your student is the cashier. You pick out an item and pay with a one-dollar, five-dollar, or ten-dollar bill; he makes change.

Use the **store cards** or items from around the house labeled with amounts less than $10 and less than $1. Ask your student to pick out two or three items that total $1 or $10.

Well, You can do part or all of Practice 3A orally. You may want to discuss problems #5 and #6 at least. Answers to practices are in the back of this guide.

 Practice 3A, p. 41

1. (a) **3** dollars, **45** cents   (b) **6** dollars, **0** cents
   (c) **7** dollars, **5** cents   (d) **0** dollars, **80** cents

2. (a) **220**   (b) **305**

3. (a) **0.75**   (b) **2.60**

US› 4. (a) **4**   (b) **4**   (c) **5**
3d› 4. (a) **10**   (b) **4**   (c) **5**

5. $1 – 85¢ = **15¢**

6. $10 - $8.60 = **$1.40**

 Material: **Store cards** (see preface) and **coins and bills**.
Procedure: Give each player four ten-dollar bills (or index cards with $10 written on them to represent ten-dollar bills) and put coins in a central pool. Shuffle and place store cards face down. Each player takes turns turning up a card, paying into the central pool for the item, and getting change from the central pool. The first player to use up all his money or to not have enough money to buy the item wins.

Workbook Exercise 30

Part 2 – Adding Money

 In this section, your student will learn the following strategies for adding money within $10.

<u>Add the dollars and then add the cents</u>. For example, add $4.15 and $3.50 by first adding $4 and $3 to get $7, then adding 15¢ and 50¢ to get 65¢; the sum is $7.65. The problems at this level will only use multiples of 5 for the cents to facilitate mental addition. Your student will be able to add the cents mentally by adding tens and then adding another five to the next ten if both numbers have fives (e.g. 35¢ + 45¢ = 35¢ + 40¢ + 5¢ = 75¢ + 5¢ = 80¢). If the cents add up to a dollar, they increase the dollar amount by 1.

<u>Use the formal algorithm for addition</u>. Write the problem vertically, aligning the dots (decimals) and add using the same methods as with whole numbers. Your student can use the formal algorithm when he cannot solve the problem mentally.

<u>Add money by first making a whole number of dollars</u>. This method can be used when the cents add to more than a dollar, particularly when it is easy to see what needs to be added to one set of money to make a whole dollar, and what remains when this is amount is subtracted from the other set of money.

$6.25 + $1.85

$6.25 + $1.85 = $7.25 + $0.85 = $8 + $0.10 = $8.10
$0.75 $0.10

<u>Add a whole number of dollars, and subtract the difference</u>. This method can be used when the cents in the amount being added are close to 100.

$6.25 + $2.95

$6.25 $\xrightarrow{+\$3}$ $9.25 $\xrightarrow{-5¢}$ $9.20

(1) Adding Cents or Dollars (p. 43)

➢ Add dollars to dollars and cents.
➢ Add cents to dollars and cents.
➢ Add cents to make $1.

 In these activities, the total money should be less than $10. Use multiples of 5 for the cents to facilitate mental addition.

Show two sets of money, one with bills and coins and one with just bills, such as $4.15 and $3. Have your student add the money by adding the dollars together. Have her write the equation.
$4.15 + $3 = $7.15

Show two sets of money, one with bills and coins and one with just coins, such as $4.15 and 35¢. Have your student add the money by adding the coins together. Have her write the equation
$4.15 + 35¢ = $4.50

Show two sets of money, one with bills and coins and one with just coins, where to coins will add up to $1, such as $4.15 and 85¢. Have your student add the money by adding the coins together. Since the coins add to a dollar, the dollar amount is increased by one.
$4.15 + 85¢ = $5

 Learning Tasks 1-3, p. 43
In learning task 3, your student should recognize that the cents make 100, or $1.

1. (a) $**6.95**   (b) $**14.45**

2. (a) **75**¢   (b) $**2.75**   (c) $**5.75**

3. (a) **$1**   (b) **$3**   (c) **$4**
    (d) **$1**   (e) **$2**   (f) **$4**

 Workbook Exercise 31

(2) Adding Cents and Dollars (pp. 42-43)

 ➢ Add dollars to dollars and cents to cents.

 Show two sets of money, both with **bills** and **coins**, such as $4.15 and $3.35. Have your student add the money by first adding the dollars, then adding the cents. Have him write the equation.

$4.15 + $3.25 = $7.50

Do an example where the second set includes dollar amounts and the cents add to $1, such as $2.60 + $4.40.

 Page 42
Learning Tasks 4-5, p. 43

$7.65

4. (a) **$6.75**, **$6.95**, **$6.95** (b) **$8.65**, **$8.80**, **$8.80**

5. (a) **$9.80**   (b) **$9.75**   (c) **$9.90**   (d) **$7.80**

 If your student is competent in mental math techniques, you may also show her how to add sets of money in which the cents add to more than $1 by making $1. This can be used in situations where it is easy to "make 100" with one of the sets of cents by subtracting that amount from the other set. For example:

$5.65 + $1.45
Add the $1 to $5.65:
$5.65 + $1.45 = $6.65 + 45¢
The difference between 65 and 100 is 35.
Take 35¢ from the 45¢ to make $1 and
increase the dollar amount by one. Add the remaining cents.

$$45¢$$
$$\overset{+35¢}{\diagup} \quad \overset{+10¢}{\diagdown}$$
$$\$6.65 \longrightarrow \$7 \longrightarrow \$7.10$$

 Workbook Exercise 32

(3) Adding Money (p. 44)

 ➢ Add money using the addition algorithm.

 Write an addition problem involving two amounts of money under $10. Write the amounts vertically one under the other, in dollars and cents, aligning the dots. Ask your student for the number of cents and rewrite the problem using cents. Tell your student that you can add the cents, and then rewrite the answer in dollars and cents. If he lines up the numbers that are being added together so that the dots are aligned, he can just work the problem as if there were no dots, and put the dot in the answer at the same place.

$$
\begin{array}{r}
\$4.78 \\
+\ \$2.69 \\
\hline
\$7.47
\end{array}
\qquad \square \qquad
\begin{array}{r}
{}^{1}\ {}^{1} \\
4\ 7\ 8 \\
+\ 2\ 6\ 9 \\
\hline
7\ 4\ 7
\end{array}
$$

Any problem where it seems mental math strategies are not easily applicable can be done using the addition algorithm. If your student needs to review the addition algorithm, provide more examples and have him trade pennies for dimes and dimes for dollars in the same manner as was done in *Primary Mathematics 2A* with number discs or base-10 blocks.

 Learning Task 6, p. 44

6.   (a) **$4.25**   (b) **$7.55**   (c) **$7.50**   (d) **$8.45**

 Workbook Exercise 33

(4) More Mental Math (p. 44)

 ➢ Add money by adding a whole number of dollars and then subtracting the difference.

 Write $3.70 + 95¢. You can set out the amount in coins and bills.

Point out that the 95¢ is almost $1.
Ask for the difference between 95¢ and $1.
Help your student see that we can add $1 and then subtract the 5¢ to get the total.
Have your student find the total this way.

$3.70 + 95¢
95¢ = $1 - 5¢

$$\$3.70 \xrightarrow{+\$1} \$4.70 \xrightarrow{-5¢} \$4.65$$

Write $3.45 + $4.97. You can show the amounts with coins and bills.
Discuss various ways of adding these amounts.
$4.97 is almost $5. If we add $5, we will be adding 3¢ too much. So we can add $5 and then subtract 3¢.

$3.45 + $4.97
4.97¢ = $5 - 3¢

$$\$3.45 \xrightarrow{+\$5} \$8.45 \xrightarrow{-3¢} \$8.42$$

 Learning Tasks 7-10, pp. 44-45

7.   (a) **$7.25, $7.20, $7.20**   (b) **$6.60, $6.59, $6.59**

8.   (a) **$4.35**   (b) **$7.60**   (c) **$6.14**   (d) **$6.24**

 You can use Mental Math 29 for more practice.

 Workbook Exercise 34

(5) Word Problems (p. 45)

 ➢ Solve word problems involving the addition of money.

 Learning Tasks 9-10, p. 45

9. The cost of the meal is one part, and the money left over the other part.
   Total money = cost of meal + money left over
   = $5.95 + $1.60 = **$7.55**

10. This is a comparison problem. One part is the cost of the toy car and the other the difference in cost.
    Cost of stuffed toy = cost of toy car + difference in cost
    = $5.70 + $3.80 = **$9.50**

➤ Set up a play store. Use **money** and the **store cards** or items from around the house labeled with amounts less than $10. Take turns being the buyer or the cashier. The buyer starts with a certain amount of money, perhaps $20. She selects two or three items, adds their cost together, and pays for the item. The cashier gives the correct change. The buyer must make sure the change is correct

Select two items without letting your student know which two (select them visually, don't pick them up), add their cost together, and give your student the total. Your student tries to determine which two items you picked.

 Material: **store cards**.

Procedure: Shuffle the cards and place face down. Players start with a total of $0. They take turns drawing cards and adding to their total. The first player that reaches a predetermined amount, perhaps $50, wins.

Part 3 – Subtracting Money

 In this section, your student will learn the following strategies for subtracting money within $10.

<u>Subtract the dollars and then the cents</u>. For example, to find the difference between $8.75 and $3.50, we first find the difference between $8 and $3, and then between 75¢ and 50¢. The problems at this level will only use multiples of 5 for the cents to facilitate mental addition. Your student will be able to subtract the cents mentally.

<u>Use the formal algorithm for subtraction</u>. Write the problem vertically, aligning the dots (decimals) and subtract using the same methods as with whole numbers. Your student can use the formal algorithm when she cannot solve the problem mentally.

<u>Subtract from a whole number of dollars</u>. This method can be used when it is easy to make 100 with the cents.

$$\$6 - 85¢$$
$$\$5 \quad \$1 - 85¢ = 15¢$$
$$\$5.15$$

<u>Subtract a whole number of dollars, and add the difference</u>. This method can be used when the cents in one set of money is close to 100.

$$\$6.25 - 2.95¢$$
$$\$6.25 \xrightarrow{\ -\$3\ } \$3.25 \xrightarrow{\ +5¢\ } \$3.30$$

(1) Subtracting Cents or Dollars (p. 47)

➢ Subtract dollars from dollars and cents.
➢ Subtract cents from dollars and cents.
➢ Subtract cents from a whole number of dollars.

Use **coins** and **bills**. The total money should be less than $10. Use multiples of 5 for the cents to facilitate mental addition.

Show a set of money; $7.85. Ask the student to subtract $3. Have him write the equation.
$7.85 – $3 = $4.85

Show a set of money; $7.85. Ask the student to subtract 30¢. Have him write the equation
$7.85 – 30¢ = $7.55

Show a set of bills; $3. Ask the student to subtract 15¢. He should recall the mental math methods in Unit 1 to "make 100" and subtract from $1 as 100¢. Have him write the equation.
$3 – 15¢ = $2.85

 Learning Tasks 1-5, p. 47

1. (a) **$5.15** (b) **$4.35** (c) **$0.80**
   (d) **$0.45** (e) **$2.45** (f) **$3.45**

2. (a) **60¢**   (b) **$2.60** (c) **$9.60**

3. (a) **$0.10** (b) **$3.40** (c) **$5.50**
   (d) **$1.25** (e) **$5.55** (f) **$6.95**

Workbook Exercise 35

---

(2) Subtracting Cents and Dollars (pp. 46-47)

 ➢ Subtract dollars from dollars and cents from cents.

 Show a set of **coins** and **bills**; $7.85. Ask the student to subtract $3.30. He should take away the dollars and then the cents. Write the equation and show how he can solve it in two steps – first subtract the dollars, and then the cents.
$7.85 – $3.30 = $5.55

 Page 46
Learning Tasks 4-5, p. 47

$**5.25**

4. (a) $**3.90**, $**3.40**, $**3.40**   (b) $**1.65**, $**1.60**, $**1.60**

5. (a) $**6.20**   (b) $**3.55**   (c) $**0.40**   (d) $**4.15**

 If your student is competent in mental math techniques, you may also show him how to subtract mentally by subtracting the dollars and then subtracting from a whole number of dollars. This can be used in situations where it is easy to "make 100" with the amount being subtracted. For example:
$5.45 – $1.75
Subtract the $1 from $5.45:
$5.45 – $1.75 = $4.45 – 75¢
The difference between 100 and 75 is 25.
Reduce the dollar amount by another dollar, and
add the 25¢.

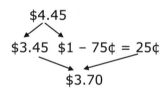

$4.45
$3.45 $1 – 75¢ = 25¢
$3.70

 Workbook Exercise 36

(3) Subtracting Money (p. 48)

 ➤ Subtract money using the subtraction algorithm.

 Help your student do some money subtraction problems using the formal algorithm. Point out that the "dots" or decimal points are aligned when writing the problem vertically.

$$
\begin{array}{r}
\$4.58 \\
- \ \underline{\$2.69} \\
\$1.89
\end{array}
\qquad \longrightarrow \qquad
\begin{array}{r}
{}^{3}\ {}^{14} \\
\cancel{4}\ \cancel{5}\ {}^{1}8 \\
- \ \underline{2\ 6\ 9} \\
1\ 8\ 9
\end{array}
$$

Any problems where it seems mental math strategies are not easily applicable can be done using the subtraction algorithm. If your student needs to review this skill, provide more examples and have him trade dimes for pennies and dollars for dimes in the same manner as was done in *Primary Mathematics 2A* with base-10 material.

 Learning Task 6, p. 48

6. (a) **$4. 80**   (b) **$3.65**
   (c) **$2.65**   (d) **$4.30**
   (e) **$1.60**   (f) **$1.65**

 Workbook Exercise 37

---

(4) More Mental Math (p. 48)

 ➤ Subtract money by subtracting a whole number of dollars and then adding back the difference.

 Write $3.70 – 95¢. Ask your student for ideas on how to subtract mentally. Since 95¢ is 5¢ less than a dollar, if we subtract $1 we are subtracting 5¢ too much. We can subtract the dollar, then add back in the 5¢.

$3.70 – 95¢
$1 = 95¢ + 5¢

$$\$3.70 \xrightarrow{-\$1} \$2.70 \xrightarrow{+5¢} \$2.75$$

Write $7.45 – $4.97. Ask your student for ideas on how to subtract mentally. We can subtract $5 and then add back in 3¢.

$7.45 – $4.97
$5 = $4.97 + 3¢

$$\$7.45 \xrightarrow{-\$5} \$2.45 \xrightarrow{+3¢} \$4.48$$

 Learning Tasks 7-8, p. 48

7.　(a) **$3.60, $3.65, $3.65**　(b) **$3.25, $3.26, $3.26**

8.　(a) **$2.50**　(b) **$2.35**
　　(c) **$3.21**　(d) **$1.01**

 You can use Mental Math 30 for more practice.

 Workbook Exercise 38

(5) Word Problems (p. 49)

  ➤ Solve word problems involving the addition and subtraction of money.

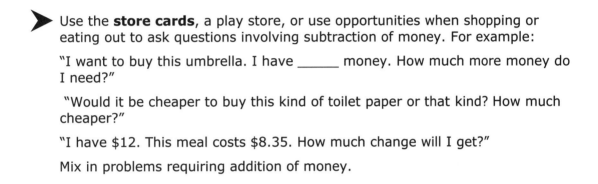 **Learning Tasks 9-10, p. 49**

   9. $**1.55**

  10. $**3.45**

➤ Use the **store cards**, a play store, or use opportunities when shopping or eating out to ask questions involving subtraction of money. For example:

"I want to buy this umbrella. I have _____ money. How much more money do I need?"

"Would it be cheaper to buy this kind of toilet paper or that kind? How much cheaper?"

"I have $12. This meal costs $8.35. How much change will I get?"

Mix in problems requiring addition of money.

 Material: **Store cards**.

Procedure: Shuffle the cards and place them in the middle face down. Players write $10 on their paper. They take turns drawing two cards each. First they find the difference between the items on the cards. They record the items and the difference in cost. Repeat 2 more times. They will have 3 differences recorded. Players then add their three values together. The student with the highest sum wins.

➤ The workbook exercises involve both addition and subtraction. If your student still needs help deciding whether to add or subtract, discuss some of the word problems in Practice 3B, p. 50. Help your student see whether both parts are given, or one part and a total.

 Workbook Exercise 39

Practice (pp. 50-51)

 ➢ Solve problems involving the addition and subtraction of money.

 Practice 3B, p. 50

1. (a) **$6**   (b) **$0.35**
2. (a) **$5.95**   (b) **$4.05**
3. (a) **$9.05**   (b) **$1.80**
4. (a) **$9.45**   (b) **$1.55**
5. (a) **$8.59**   (b) **$3.15**
6. Total cost = $1.40 + $7.85 = **$9.25**
7. Amount slippers cost less than shoes = $10 - $6.30 = **$3.70**
8. Change received = $5 - $1.85 = **$3.15**
9. Amount of money = $4.25 + $1.95 = **$6.20**
10. Amount of money = $5.65 + $1.70 = **$7.35**

 Practice 3C, p. 51

1. (a) **$10**   (b) **$0.35**
2. (a) **$9.35**   (b) **$1.90**
3. (a) **$9.55**   (b) **$1.30**
4. (a) **$10. 20** (b) **$1.65**
5. (a) **$9.75**   (a) **$0.06**
6. Amount of money he had at first = $6.80 + $2.40 = **$9.20**
7. Total spent = $1.95 + $1.60 = **$3.55**
8. Amount saved the second week = $6.45 - $3.95 = **$2.50**
9. Cost of belt = $8.05 - $1.90 = **$6.15**
10. Money left = $9.20 - $2.80 = **$6.40**

Review

 ➤ Review all topics

 There are two reviews in the workbook. You can use the first to see if any topics need reteaching.

For a lesson, you can use this opportunity to also review multiplication and division. You can do some of the games from that section, the mental math pages, or other resources such as web sites.

Use the appendix page 35 in this guide to review U.S. measurement. Answers are given here.

1. (a) yd   (b) in   (c) ft   (d) yd

2. (a) lb   (b) oz   (c) lb   (d) lb

3. 62 lb – 14 lb = 48 lb

4. (a) 15 oz – 3 oz = 12 oz   (b) 12 oz ÷ 2 oz = 6

 Workbook Review 3
Workbook Review 4

Unit 4 – Fractions

Part 1 – Halves and Quarters

(1) Halves and Quarters (pp. 52-53)

- ➢ Recognize one half and one fourth.
- ➢ Read and write the fractional notation for $\frac{1}{2}$ and $\frac{1}{4}$.

 Students were introduced to halves and quarters in *Primary Mathematics 1B*. This is reviewed here and the fractional notation for $\frac{1}{2}$ and $\frac{1}{4}$ is introduced here. Your student should understand that $\frac{1}{2}$ of a whole means one out of two equal parts and $\frac{1}{4}$ of a whole means one out of four equal parts. Two halves make a whole and four quarters make a whole.

➤ Ask the student what he would do if he wanted to share four cookies equally between himself and a friend? He would divide them evenly. How would he share two cookies? What about one cookie? He would have to divide it into two equal pieces and give himself and his friend each a half. Ask him whether, if he gave his friend a little bit off of the cookie, he would be giving a half. No, both pieces must be the same size.

halves

not halves

➤ Use sheets of paper. Show your student how to fold one of them in half. She must line up the corners and edges in order to get equal halves. Show her how to make a sharp crease. Unfold and color half.

Ask her how much is colored. Write $\frac{1}{2}$. Explain that this is read as "one-half" and means 1 out of 2 equal pieces. Tell her a part of something can also be called a *fraction* of something. $\frac{1}{2}$ is a fraction. Let her try some other ways to divide the paper in half.

Now show her how to fold a piece of paper in fourths, by
first folding in half and then again in half, along the same
side. Unfold and have her color a quarter. Ask her how
much is colored. Write $\frac{1}{4}$.

This is read as "one-fourth" or "one quarter" and means 1 out of 4 equal pieces.
$\frac{1}{2}$ and $\frac{1}{4}$ are both different fractions of the paper.

Cut the colored pieces out from the paper folded in half and the one folded in
fourths and put them on top of each other. Ask which is larger.

Point out that when we talk about one-half or one-fourth, we are always talking
about one-half of *something* or one-fourth of *something*. When we saw that the
half was larger than the fourth, they were both fractions of the same sized
thing, the piece of paper. When we compare fractions, they have to be fractions
of the same sized thing. One fourth of a large piece of paper could be the same
size as one half of a smaller piece of paper.

Let her try some other ways to divide the paper into quarters.

Copy and cut the circle in the appendix. Have your student try folding it into
halves and quarters.

 pp. 52-53
Learning Tasks 1-2, p. 53

1. (a) **B, D**   (b) **P, Q**

2. (a) **2**   (b) **4**

 Workbook Exercise 40

Part 2 – Writing Fractions

(1) Fractional Notation (pp. 54-55)

➢ Understand fractional notation.

Students have already learned about part-whole in both addition and multiplication. In addition, two or more unequal parts can make the whole, or total. In multiplication, a given number of equal parts make the whole, or total.

Fractions also represent a part-whole relationship. The fraction notation tells how much of the whole the part represents. $\frac{1}{4}$ represents 1 out of 4 equal parts of the whole. $\frac{3}{4}$ represents 3 out of 4 equal parts.

Students will later learn that the whole can be any amount, such as 24, and will find $\frac{1}{4}$ of the whole by first finding the value of each equal part using division. For now, the whole is simply one unit, whether a cookie, a pizza, a fraction bar, or a circle.

➤ Copy the **fraction circles** and the unlabeled **fraction bars** in the appendix (or use commercially available fraction circles).

Cut out the circle divided into sixths. Have your student color one section. Ask him how much he has colored (one sixth). Write $\frac{1}{6}$. One out of 6 of the parts is colored. Ask him to color another part. Ask him how many parts are colored (two sixths). Write $\frac{1}{6} + \frac{1}{6} = \frac{2}{6}$. One sixth and one sixth are two sixths. Ask him what $\frac{1}{6}$ means (2 out of 6 equal parts). Continue until all the parts are colored.

Repeat with one of the fraction strips and a different fraction.

➤ Write some fractions up to 12/12, and ask students to name them. Except for one half, we say the top number as a regular counting number, and the bottom the same way we say the position in line (e.g. third, fourth, fifth) except that we add an "s". So $\frac{3}{5}$ is "three fifths." A four on the bottom can be either fourths or quarters. $\frac{3}{4}$ can be either "three fourths" or "three quarters."

p. 54
Learning Tasks 1-2, p. 55

1. (a) **1, 5**   (b) **4, 5**

2. (a) $\frac{1}{6}$ (b) **3, 8,** $\frac{3}{8}$

 Workbook Exercise 41

(2) Writing Fractions (p. 56)

➢ Identify and write different fractions of a whole.

➤ Use some of the cut out **fraction circles** and **fraction bars**.

Color parts of them, and ask your student to write the fraction that is colored. Write a fraction. Ask your student to pick out the correct circle or strip and color the correct number of parts show the fraction. He does not have to color contiguous parts.

The parts colored do not have to be contiguous. For example:

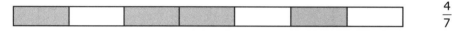 $\frac{4}{7}$

If you have connect-a-cube geo-shapes, you can make different shapes of 2 different colors and ask yours student for the fraction that is one of the colors.

Learning Tasks 3-4, pp. 55-56

3. (a) $\frac{3}{7}$ (b) $\frac{5}{6}$

4. (a) $\frac{4}{9}$ (b) $\frac{4}{6}$ (c) $\frac{3}{8}$ (d) $\frac{7}{10}$

Workbook Exercises 42-43

(3) Comparing Fractions (p. 57)

 ➢ Compare unit fractions.

 When a whole is divided into equal parts, a unit fraction is one of the parts. $\frac{1}{4}$ and $\frac{1}{6}$ are unit fractions. We can compare unit fractions by comparing the denominator. The more parts the whole is divided into, the larger the denominator, and the smaller the part. $\frac{1}{6}$ is smaller than $\frac{1}{4}$ because the part of the whole is smaller.

➤ Tell your student that 6 people want to share a pizza. Draw a circle and divide it into 6 pieces. Then tell him that 4 people want to share a pizza of the same size. Draw another circle the same size and divide it into 4 pieces. Ask who would get a larger piece, someone in the first group or someone in the second group? Why? Since the first pizza has to be cut up into more pieces, each piece is smaller.

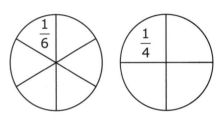

$\frac{1}{4}$ is greater than $\frac{1}{6}$

Write $\frac{1}{4}$ is greater than $\frac{1}{6}$.

➤ Copy the unlabelled **fraction bars** in the appendix. Cut out the strips. Give the strips to your student and have her color one part of each strip on the left side, write the fraction the colored part represents, and arrange the strips in order one on top of the other. Ask them which is smaller, $\frac{1}{8}$ or $\frac{1}{10}$. If the whole is divided into more parts, each part will be smaller. Do some other examples.

➤ Write down 3 or more unit fractions, and have her put them in order from smallest to greatest without the help of the fraction strips.

 Learning Tasks 5-6, p. 57

5. $\frac{1}{4}$

6. $\frac{1}{8}$, $\frac{1}{5}$, $\frac{1}{2}$

 Workbook Exercise 44

(4) Making a Whole (p. 57)

 ➢ Find fractions which together make a whole.

 Draw a fraction circle grid, square, or bar. Color in part of it. Or you can use two different colors of linking cubes or connect-a-cubes. Ask your student for the fraction that is colored. Then ask her for the fraction that is not colored. Ask what both fractions together make.

Write the two fractions that make a whole. Ask her to add the top numbers (the number of parts) together and compare the sum to the bottom number.

Repeat with a few other examples.

$\frac{4}{9}$ and $\frac{5}{9}$ make 1 whole

 Learning Task 7, p. 57

7. (a) $\frac{2}{5}$ (b) $\frac{6}{7}$ (c) $\frac{7}{9}$

 Material: A set of cards with the following fractions: $\frac{1}{2}, \frac{1}{2}, \frac{1}{3}, \frac{2}{3}, \frac{1}{4}, \frac{2}{4}, \frac{2}{4},$

$\frac{3}{4}, \frac{1}{5}, \frac{2}{5}, \frac{3}{5}, \frac{4}{5}, \frac{1}{6}, \frac{2}{6}, \frac{3}{6}, \frac{3}{6}, \frac{4}{6}, \frac{5}{6}, \frac{1}{7}, \frac{2}{7}, \frac{3}{7}, \frac{4}{7}, \frac{5}{7}, \frac{6}{7}, \frac{1}{8}, \frac{2}{8}, \frac{3}{8}, \frac{4}{8},$

$\frac{4}{8}, \frac{5}{8}, \frac{6}{8}, \frac{7}{8}, \frac{1}{9}, \frac{2}{9}, \frac{3}{9}, \frac{4}{9}, \frac{5}{9}, \frac{6}{9}, \frac{7}{9},$ and $\frac{8}{9}$.

Procedure: Shuffle the cards and place face down. Place the top two cards face up on the table. Players take turns drawing cards. If the player can match his card to a card on the table to make a whole, he gets to keep both cards. If not, he places the card he drew face up on the table. The player with the most cards after all the cards have been turned up wins.

 Workbook Exercise 45

Review

 ➤ Review previous material.

➤ **Enrichment**
Give your student a piece of string. Ask him how he can cut it into 4 equal pieces. He can fold it in half, cut at the fold, and then fold each piece in half again and cut at the fold. Ask him how many places the string had to be cut in order to cut it into four pieces. It was cut in 3 places. Ask him how many places the string would be cut to cut it into five equal pieces? (4) 6 equal pieces? (5) Twenty equal pieces? (19).

➤ **Enrichment**
Draw a picture of a circular cake, or use a real cake (don't show him the ones drawn here). Ask your student how many cuts he would use to cut it into two equal pieces. (1) Four equal pieces? (2) Eight equal pieces? (4) 16 equal pieces? (8)

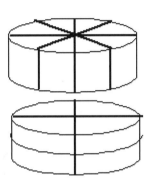

Challenge her to figure out a way of cutting it into eight pieces with only 3 cuts. If she needs help, remind her of the different ways of dividing the paper into halves. What is another way she can cut the cake in half?

➤ Do some or all of review B and C with your student; have your student do the rest independently.

 Review B, p. 58

1. (a) **833**   (b) **300**   (c) **479**

2. (a) **505**   (b) **101**   (c) **127**

3. (a) **24**   (b) **50**   (c) **24**

4. (a) **4**   (b) **9**   (c) **9**

5. Difference in height = 132 cm – 119 cm = **13 cm**

6. Cost of television set = $800 - $398 = **$402**

7. Total money saved = $3 x 5 = **$15**

8. Total distance = 450 m + 365 m = **815 m**

9. Amount of change = $5 - $2.45 = **$2.55**

Review C, p. 59

1. (a) **562**   (b) **397**   (c) **448**

2. (a) **269**   (b) **231**   (c) **19**

3. (a) **35**   (b) **90**   (c) **32**

4. (a) **9**   (b) **5**   (c) **6**

5. (a) **208**   (b) **530**   (c) **194**   (d) **283**

6. Difference = 520 – 485 = **35**

7. Number of stamps Ali collected = 735 + 65 = **800**

8. Number of bags = 27 kg ÷ 3 kg = **9**

9. Total length = 6 x 5 m = **30 m**

10. Total number of batteries = 6 x 4 = **24**

Unit 5 – Time

Part 1 – Telling Time

(1) Time to 5 Minutes (pp. 60-62)

➢ Tell time as minutes after or before the hour.

 Students learned to tell time to the hour and half-hour and to read and say the time as "4 o'clock" or "half past 4" in *Primary Mathematics 1B*. Here, they will learn to tell time to the five-minute interval, and to read and write time using the hour:minutes notation (e.g. 7:05). You can extend the concepts in this section to telling time to the minute.

3d› In the U.S. a colon is used between the hour and the minutes. That convention will be followed in this guide. If you are using the 3d edition and want to use the same convention used there (a dot between the hour and minutes) use it instead in the discussions with your student.

Students may be more familiar with a digital clock. An analog clock, or "face" clock, will give them a visual picture of time and the fraction of an hour that has passed. It is also useful in determining time intervals. Use a face clock with geared hands.

➤ Use a **clock with geared hands**. Remind your student which hand is the hour hand and which is the minute hand. Ask him what the numbers around the clock mean (the hours).

Set the time for 12:00 and move the minute hand all the way around. Ask your student how far the hour hand goes when the minute hand goes all the way around. One hour passes as the minute hand goes around, and the hour changes to the next hour. Have your student tell you some events that take about an hour.

Review telling time to the hour and the half-hour. Set the time to an hour, such as 4:00, and ask your student for the time. She may have learned this as "4 o'clock" in *Primary Mathematics 1B*. Move the hand around half-way. Ask her how far around the hand moved. Ask her for the time. She may have learned this is "half past 4." Ask her to set the clock for given times on the hour or half-hour.

➤ Get your student to count the number of small intervals between two numbers marked by the small lines. Tell him that when the minute hand on a real clock moves from one small mark to the next one minute has passed. If you have a real analog clock, let him watch it until the hand moves. There are 5 minutes between one number (larger mark) and the next. Start the minute hand at 12 and have him count by 5 as you move it from number to number. He will find that there are 60 minutes in an hour.

 Page 60

Discuss this page with your student.

▶ Help your student to get a feel for the time duration of one minute. Use a stopwatch and time some activity, such as hopping in place, for 1 minute.

▶ Set the time on an hour, such as 6:00 and ask students for the time. Write it down using the digital notation. Tell your student that this is how we can write 6 o'clock. The colon (or dot in the 3d edition of *Primary Mathematics*) separates the hours from the minutes. When the minute hand is straight up, no minutes have passed for the hour yet, so the minutes are 00.

6:00
"6 o'clock"

Move the minute hand to the 1. Ask how many minutes this is. Write the time as 6:05. Tell your student we read this as "six oh five" and it means "5 minutes after 6 o'clock", or "5 minutes past 6." Point out that as with money (e.g. the cents in $6.05) we need to have two digits for the minutes, so if there are no tens we put in 0 as a place holder.

6:05
"six oh five"
"five minutes past 6"

Continue around the clock for every five minutes. Point out that the hour hand is moving slowly around as well, and that at 6:30 it is halfway to the 7. 6:30 is read as "six thirty" and is "30 minutes after 6" or "half past six."

 Page 61

▶ Set the time at various times (multiples of 5) and have your student read and write the time in the digital format.

Write some times in the digital format and have your student set the correct times on the clock.

6:45

➤ Set the time on the clock to a half-hour, such as 2:30. Tell your student this is also 30 minutes to 3. Count by fives from the 6 to 12 to show that there are 30 more minutes to go. Move the minute hand to 2:35, write the time, and have your student count by fives from the minute hand position to the 12. Tell her that this time can also be given as "25 minutes before 3 o'clock" or 25 minutes to 3." Point out that 25 minutes + 35 minutes = 60 minutes, or one hour. Continue with 2:40, 2:45, 2:50, and 2:55.

2:35
35 minutes past 2
25 minutes to 2

➤ Draw a circle and divide it into quarters. Write 12, 3, 6, and 9 at each quarter. Use the clock and set the time at 12:00. Move the minute hand to 3. Outline the quarter circle with your finger. Tell your student that the minute hand has moved a quarter of the way around. This time is also called "a quarter past 12."

12:15
a quarter past 12

Move the minute hand to the 9. Ask your student for the time. This time is "twelve forty-five", "15 minutes to 1", "a quarter to one."

12:45
a quarter to 1

 Learning Task 1, p. 62

1.   (a) **5**   (b) **30**   (c) **15**   (d) **5**

➤ Usually when people look at a clock they only need to approximate time to the nearest five minutes. You may want to extend this discussion to telling time to the minute. Set the time to some time between the five minute intervals and show your student that he can count the minutes by fives until he gets to the number just before the minute hand position, and then by ones to the minute hand position.

 Workbook Exercise 46

(2) Time of Day (p. 63)

➢ Relate daily activities to the time.
➢ Understand the abbreviations a.m. and p.m.

 Use a **clock with geared hands**. Show the time 12:00. Tell your student that this is 12 midnight, which is the middle of the night.

Go through various regular activities of the day in order, such as getting up, eating meals, etc. Have her show the time for each activity by moving only the minute hand until the correct time. She should note that the hours go from 12:00 midnight to 12:00 again at noon, the middle of the day. After she shows her bed-time, continue moving the minute hand around to 12. Tell her this is now 12:00 midnight again. A new day starts.

Explain to your student that we use a.m. to stand for the times between 12:00 midnight and 12:00 noon and we use p.m. to stand for the times between 12:00 noon and 12:00 midnight. Pick an activity that could be done in the morning or in the evening, for example at 8:00. Tell your student that in order to be able to tell which part of the day it is happening, you would have to say 8:00 a.m. if it was happening in the morning, or 8:00 p.m. if it was happening in the evening. Write the times down, followed by a.m. or p.m.

Ask her how many hours there are from 12:00 midnight to 12:00 noon (12) and from 12:00 noon to 12:00 midnight (12). Ask how many hours there are in the day? (24)

You may want to tell your student that many countries, and the military, use 24 hours rather than 12 hours, and don't use a.m. or p.m. So 1:00 p.m. is 13:00.

 Learning Task 2, p. 63
Have your student read and write the times. She can give different ways of reading the times, e.g. "six forty-five" or "a quarter to seven."

2. **6:00**; **6:05**; **6:20**; **6:45**; **7:15**; **7:50**

 Workbook Exercise 47

Part 2 – Time Intervals

(1) Time Intervals (pp. 64-67)

 ➢ Determine time intervals using clocks.

Your student will learn how to determine the duration of a time interval in either hours or minutes in this section, always with the use of a clock face to help them at this level. In *Primary Mathematics 3* they will learn to find the time interval without a clock face.

The times in this unit are all multiples of 5. Your student will probably be able to easily tell time to the minute, as well, but usually he will want to tell time to the nearest 5 minutes (e.g. *about* 2:25 for 2:23) rather than counting the minutes between each 5-minute interval, since an exact time is not always necessary.

➤ Use a **clock with geared hands**. Choose a familiar activity with a time interval of less than an hour. Write down the start time and the end time. Show the start time on the clock. Have your student move the minute hand and count by fives until the ending time. Ask how long the activity lasts.

➤ Show 4:10. Keep the minute hand there, and count by fives, pointing to each number, until 30 minutes. Show that the minute hand would end up opposite the start time. Try other 30 minute intervals; the minute hand always moves to a number opposite the starting time.

start 2:10   end 2:25
5, 10, 15, 20, 25
time passed = 25 minutes

Show 4:10 again. Keep a finger there, and move the minute hand to the opposite side. Write the time. (4:40) Ask how much time has passed. (30 minutes) Move the minute hand back 5 minutes. Ask how much time would have passed at that time. (25 minutes). Write the time (4:35). Point out that rather than counting by fives to 25, he can recognize which position is opposite the starting position, which would be 30 minutes, and then count back by one five.

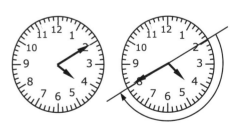

start 4:10   end 4:40
time passed = 30 minutes

Show 4:10 again. Keep a finger there, and move the minute hand to the opposite side. Move the minute hand forward another 5 minutes so that the time is 4:45. Help your student see that she can determine the time interval by seeing that the minute hand is now 5 more than half-way around the clock, so the time interval is 35 minutes. She does not have to count by fives starting at the beginning.

➤ Show 4:45. Move the hand to 5:00. Ask how much time has passed. Point out that the hand moved a quarter of the way around the circle, 3 numbers, and a quarter of an hour is 15 minutes.

 Page 64
Point out the two clocks. Help your student find the start time on the second clock and count clockwise by fives until the end time.

 Learning Task 1, p. 65
The student can mark the start time on the "End" clock with his finger, and count by fives to the end time. Encourage, but don't require, him to see alternative ways, such as counting on or back from half-way around, or seeing that a quarter of an hour has passed (15 minutes).

1.   (a) **25 min**   (b) **15 min**   (c) **25 min**   (d) **30 min**

➤ Use a **clock with geared hands**. Show a starting time of 4:00. Write the time, 4:00. Hold your finger at the number the hour hand is on, and move the minute hand all the way around once. Write the time, 5:00. Ask your student how much time has passed. (60 minutes or 1 hour) Remind her that 60 minutes is 1 hour. Point out that the minutes are the same on both the start time and the end time, but the hours have changed. Move it around one more time. Write the time, 6:00. Have your student give the number of hours that have passed.

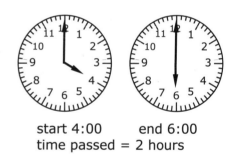

start 4:00   end 6:00
time passed = 2 hours

Set the time for 2:30. Move the minute hand around once as your student counts by fives until he gets to 60. Ask your student what the time is (3:30). Ask your student how much time has passed. 60 minutes is the same as one hour, so one hour has passed. Point out that again the minutes have not changed between the start and end time, just the hours. Go around with the minute hand another two full times. Ask your

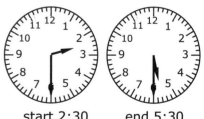

start 2:30   end 5:30
time passed = 3 hours

student how much time has now passed. Write 5:30. The minute hand is at the same place where it started, and the hour hand has moved forward 3 hours, from between 2 and 3 to between 5 and 6. So three hours have passed.

 Learning Tasks 2-4, p. 66 - 67
For task 2, the student should notice that the minute hand stays in the same place, but the hour hand changes, so the minute hand must have gone all the way around, which is an hour. In 3(a) you can point out that the minute hand changes, and so does the hour hand, but it does not go past another hour mark.

2. **60** min

3. (a) **25 min**   (b) **6 h**

4. **30** min

 Workbook Exercise 48

(2) Start and End Times (p. 67)

 ➤ Find start or end times for time intervals.

 Only a few English speaking countries still use notations with hours between 1 and 12 and additions like "a.m." and "p.m." The common 24 h international standard notation is more widely used now. The 12 h notation is hardly ever used on Continental Europe to write or display a time. Most other languages don't even have abbreviations like "a.m." and "p.m." Even in the U.S., the military and computer programmers have been using the 24 hour notation for a long time, and digital clocks can be set to display time in 24 hour notation. The abbreviation a.m. stands for ante meridian (before meridian) and p.m. stands for post meridian (after meridian).

 Learning Tasks 4-6, p. 67

5. **8:35**   6. **8:45**

➤ Remind your student that the times from 12:00 midnight to 12:00 noon are labeled with a.m., and the times from 12:00 noon to 12:00 midnight are labeled with p.m. So 4:00 a.m. would be in the morning before he gets up, and 4:00 p.m. would be in the afternoon.

Use a **clock with geared hands**. Show 11:00. Say it is 11:00 a.m., or 11:00 in the morning. Write 11:00 a.m. Move the minute hand around once. Ask your student the time. It is 12:00 noon. Move the minute hand around again, and ask your student the time. If he says 1:00, ask him whether it is in the morning or afternoon. Write 1:00 p.m. In going from 11:00 a.m. to two hours later, he must first go one hour to 12:00, then start counting from 0 for the next hour. He can do this with his fingers – hold up one finger and say 12, then the next and say 1. Two hours have passed; it is 1:00 p.m. You can also show this on a number line which starts over again at 12:

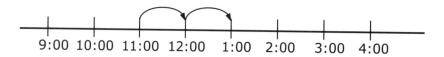

9:00 10:00 11:00 12:00   1:00 2:00   3:00 4:00

Show 10:40 and write 10:40 p.m. Ask your student to show you 5 hours later. Ask whether it is a.m. or p.m. (3:40 a.m.). He can use his fingers and count: 11:40, 12:40, 1:40, 2:40, 3:40, or he can count the hours and then add on the minutes: 11, 12, 1, 2, 3, 3:40

Ask your student to show 2:40 on the clock. Then ask him to show 30 minutes later. Ask him the time. Write 3:10. Note that the hour has changed because the minute hand moved past the 12. There are 20 minutes to the hour, and 10 after. He can count by fives as he moves the hand around until he gets to thirty. In the workbook pages, he can do it by moving his finger along for every five minutes. Do some other examples. Your student either moves the minute hand back while counting by fives, or leaves the minute hand where it is and points to each number as he counts.

Some students may want to mentally count on from the time by fives for the correct number of fives to find the end time. So if asked to find 30 minutes after 2:40, your student may write end time as 2:70. Remind your student that the minutes can never be more than 60. If he counts by fives to get the end time, rather than moving the clock hand and reading the end time, he needs to start over at 0 when he gets to 60 and count the correct number of fives. He can use his fingers to keep track of the number of fives. There are 6 fives in 30 minutes, so he can count "2:45, 2:50, 3:00, 3:05, 3:10." At this level, the student will always be able to refer to a clock face.

➤ Show a time on the clock, such as 4:30. Ask your student to supply the time a specified number of minutes or hours before, or after. Let him check his answer by moving the minute hand. Include times where the hour changes. For example, what time is 25 minutes after 4:30? (4:55) What time is 30 minutes after 4:55? (5:25) What time is 3 hours before 5:25? (2:55) Include a.m. and p.m. when doing hours.

 Workbook Exercise 49

(3) Practice (p. 68)

 ➤ Practice using and telling time.

 Practice 5A, p. 68

1. (a) **minutes**

   (b) **hours**

   (c) **hours**

   (d) **minutes**

   (e) **hours**

2. **40 min**

3. **10:10**

Review

 ➤ Review topics learned so far.

➤ Use Practice 5A and Review D to review topics learned so far in Primary Mathematics. You can do some or all of the problems as a lesson or have your student do them independently.

➤ You may want to use a globe and discuss different time zones. For example, if you live on the west coast of the US, the time in Singapore is nine hours earlier. If it is 3:00 p.m. where you live now, what time is it in Singapore? If there is a relative who lives in a different time zone, you can talk about what time it would be there, and what the relative would be doing at that time.

➤ Review multiplication and division facts for 2, 3, 4, 5, and 10, if necessary.

 Review D, p. 69

1. (a) **92**   (b) **671**   (c) **178**

2. (a) **371**   (b) **65**   (c) **425**

3. (a) **25**   (b) **24**   (c) **90**

4. (a) **9**   (b) **9**   (c) **5**

5. (a) **$9**   (b) **$1.50**   (c) **$0.45**

6. Length of each piece = total length ÷ number of pieces = 36 m ÷ 4 = **9 m**

7. (a) Number of men = total – number of women = 358 – 169 = **189**
    (b) Difference = Number of men – number of women = 189 – 169 = **20**

8. Total paid = number of tickets x price of each ticket = 5 x $7 = **$35**

9. (a) Total spent = $1.80 + $7.95 = **$9.75**
    (b) Change = $10 – $9.75 = **$0.25**

 Workbook Review 5

Unit 6 – Capacity

Part 1 – Comparing Capacity

(1) Comparing Capacity (pp. 70-71)

 ➢ Compare the capacity of containers.

 The capacity of a container is how much liquid it will hold.

Your student will learn various ways of comparing the capacity of two or more containers. She should have concrete experience actually filling up and pouring out from various containers.

There are several ways to compare the capacity of two containers.

- Fill up one container, and then pour the water from it into the other. If there is some remaining in the first when the second is full, the first has a greater capacity.
- Fill up each container, and pour the contents into smaller containers of equal capacity to see how many more small containers one fills than the other.
- Fill up both containers and pour the contents into two larger containers of equal size and shape and compare the levels.

 Use **3-4 containers** of different capacity and some smaller containers of equal capacity, such as paper cups.

Tell your student that *capacity* is the total amount of liquid a container can hold. Show him two of the containers with similar capacity and ask him which holds more water, or has the greatest capacity. Use ones where he cannot just look at them and be sure they have the same capacity – one might be taller and thinner than the other. Ask him how he can be sure of his answer. Allow him to demonstrate his ideas.

 Page 70
This illustrates one method of comparing the capacity, which is to fill up one container with water, then pour the water from it into the other.

Put different amounts of water into 3-4 cups of the same shape and size. Ask your student how she knows which one has the largest amount. She can tell by the level of the water.

Discuss another method for comparing capacity, if your student has not already suggested it. She can fill up the two containers and then pour the water from each into two larger containers of the same size and compare the level of water.

 Use 3-4 containers of different shape. Have your student fill the smallest one completely with water, and then pour that water into another container. Repeat for all the containers, and then fill the first again. Ask him which has the most water. (They all have the same amount.) Ask him whether the level of water is the same. (No) Discuss why the levels are not the same, even though they have the same amount of water.

 Learning task 1-2, p. 71
Task 1 illustrates a third method for comparing capacities, which is to fill both containers, and pour the contents into smaller containers of equal capacity. The jug holds 5 glasses of water, and the bottle holds 3 glasses of water, so the jug holds more water.

1.   **5, 3**

2.   **B, A**

 Workbook Exercises 50-51

Part 2 – Liters

(1) Liters (pp. 72-75)

➢ Understand the liter as a unit of measurement.
➢ Estimate and measure the capacity of containers in liters.
➢ Compare the capacity of containers in liters.

The SI unit (international standard unit of measurement) of volume is the cubic meter. Most countries, however, measure volume in liters.
1,000 liters = 1 cubic meter.
1 decimeter is 10 centimeters, or one tenth of a meter.
So one liter is equal to a cubic decimeter.

Liter can be abbreviated with a cursive ℓ or a capital L.

3d› The US spelling for liter will be used in this guide.

▶ Show your student a 1-liter beaker or measuring cup. Explain that most countries measure volume in liters. Show your student how to fill the measuring cup or beaker to the line marked as a liter in order to measure one liter.

▶ Use several containers. Ask your student to first estimate the number of liters and then measure by filling up the container from the measuring cup.

Page 72
Learning Tasks 1-6, pp. 73-76

1.   The jug holds the most, the glass holds the least

2.   **1 liter**

3.   (a) **B**   (b) **3 liters** more

5.   **4**

US› Workbook Exercise 52
3d› Workbook Exercises 52-53

| (2) Practice 6A, Word Problems (p. 76) |

 ➢ Solve word problems involving liters.

 Practice 6A, p. 76
Discuss these problems with your student.

1. (a) A
    (b) 12 – 8 = 4. A holds **4** ℓ more.

2. Amount of paint used = 20 ℓ – 4 ℓ = **16** ℓ

3. Amount sold in 2 weeks = 52 ℓ + 38 ℓ = **90** ℓ

4. Total milk drunk = 6 ℓ + 4 ℓ + 2 ℓ = **12** ℓ

5. Water needed = 30 ℓ – 12 ℓ = **18** ℓ

6. Number of jugs needed = 18 ÷ 3 = **6**

 US› Workbook Exercise 53
3d› Workbook Exercise 54

US› Part 3 – Gallons, Quarts, Pints and Cups

(1) Gallons, Quarts, Pints, and Cups (US› pp. 77-80)

> ➤ Understand the gallon, quart, pint, and cup as units of measurement.
> ➤ Estimate and measure the capacity of containers in gallons, quarts, pints, or cups.
> ➤ Compare gallons, quarts, pints, and cups to each other.
> ➤ Compare quart to liter.

If your student lives in the U.S., he is likely familiar with the standard units for liquid measurement used in the U.S. A quart is slightly less than a liter (about one twentieth less: 1 quart = 0.964 liters)

Your student should be able to estimate whether a container has one or several cups, or one or several quarts, or one or several gallons, and which unit would be appropriate for finding the capacity of the container. A bathtub, for example, would have a capacity in gallons, whereas a drinking cup would have a capacity in cups.

➤ Tell your student that in the U.S. we often use gallons, quarts, pints, and cups to measure liquids, especially in cooking and shopping. Metric measurements (e.g. liters, kilograms, meter, etc.) are used in science even in the U.S.

Show your student some gallon, half-gallon, quart, pint, and cup containers. You can have her find out how many cups are in a pint, pints in a quart, quarts in a half-gallon, and half-gallons in a gallon.

2 cups = 1 pint
2 pints = 1 quart
2 quarts = 1 half-gallon
2 half-gallons = 1 gallon

Use a quart measuring cup and show your student the marks for cups. Help your student fill the measuring cup up to the one or two cup marks, or quart mark. Most such measuring cups also show liters. Have your student compare the mark for liter with that for quart. A liter is just a little bit more than a quart.

➤ You can have your student estimate the capacity of a container in cups, pints, or quarts in a container and then measure.

➤ Cooking is a good place to discuss and use standard U.S. fluid measurements.

US> Pages 77-78
Learning Tasks 1-5, US> pp. 78-80

2. The larger one on the left

3. **quart**

4. (a) **no**   (b) **yes**

5. (a) **gallon** (b) **pint, cup**   (c) **cup, pint**   (d) **quart**

 US> Workbook Exercise 54

Review

 ➢ Review all topics

 Review E, US› p. 81, 3d› p. 77

1. (a) **825**   (b) **600**   (c) **800**

2. (a) **301**   (b) **146**   (c) **199**

3. (a) **32**   (b) **30**   (c) **80**

4. (a) **6**   (b) **10**   (c) **9**

US›
3d› 5. (a) **$6.30**   (b) **$6.01**   (c) **$1.85**
        (a) **$6**

6. Amount each girl paid = $28 ÷ 4 = **$7**

7. Cost of the book = $5.80 + $2.75 = **$8.55**

8. Total liters = 5 ℓ x 7 = **35 ℓ**

9. **11:20 a.m.**

10. (a) Number of children = 203 – 128 = **75**
     (b) Number more adults than children = 128 – 75 = **53**

Unit 7 – Graphs

Part 1 – Picture Graphs

(1) Picture Graphs I (US› pp. 82-85, 3d› pp. 78-81)

 ➢ Create and interpret scaled picture graphs.

 In *Primary Mathematics 1*, students learned to interpret picture graphs where one symbol represented one item being graphed. Here your student will learn to create and interpret picture graphs where one symbol represents more than one item. The scale used should be 2, 3, 4, 5, or 10. This will reinforce the multiplication facts learned earlier.

At this stage, students will not be using partial symbols to represent ½ or ¼.

While doing this unit, you can teach your student how to tally. Tallying is used to keep track of counts when it is not easy to remember the last counted number, or when trying to keep track of the number of several things at once, such as when counting car colors or bird species. To tally, one mark is made for each count. Every fifth mark is drawn across the previous four. The total can be found by counting by fives or tens.

 US› pp. 82-84, 3d› pp. 78-80
Your student can count the fruit and see that the number of symbols in the graph is the same as the number of fruit. Ask your student which page is easiest to use to compare the number of each kind of fruit, i.e. which fruit there is the most of, and how much more than the other kinds of fruit. The graph on p. 84 represents the same data as the one on p. 83, except that this time each symbol stands for 2 fruit.

4 types, **12** mangoes, **6** pears, **8** apples, **4** oranges, **30** total

> (a) **2 fruit** (b) **12 fruit** (c) **2**
> (d) **4** (e) **mango** (f) **orange**

➤ Use objects such as counters or multilink cubes where there are several colors.

Start with less than ten of each color. Have your student group them and line them up according to the color as they would in a picture graph. If he wants, he can construct a picture graph. Then use more than ten of each color. Select quantities such that the numbers of each color are multiples of 2, 3, or 5. List the different colors. Have him select one counter or cube at a time and call out its color while you tally them. Show him how you make one mark for each color, and when there is a fifth one you cross the previous four marks:

Red |||| |||

Green |||

etc.

Finish by letting him make the tally marks as you call out each color. Then have him count by fives and give the total for each color.

Ask him how he would create a picture graph to show how many he had of each that could fit on one sheet of paper. He can make very small pictures, or he can let one picture stand for more than one object. Guide him to select an appropriate number of objects the picture can represent (Avoid cases where the resulting picture graph would require a fraction of an object, for example, there are 6 of one color. A scale of 1 to 4 would be inappropriate, since half a picture would be needed for 2 objects.) Draw the columns for a graph for him, discuss how it can be labeled, and have him draw a symbols. There should be a label for each color and a key to tell the value of each symbol. The graph should have a title, such as "The Number of Each Color of Counter." Point out that the graph can be vertical or horizontal. If he is interested, give him other opportunities to make graphs.

Learning Task 1, US› p. 85, 3d› p. 81

1.   (a) **15**   (b) **12**   (c) **5**   (d) **zoo**   (e) **9**

Workbook Exercises 55-56

(2) Picture Graphs II (US› pp. 86-87, 3d› pp. 82-83)

 ➤ Interpret scaled picture graphs.

 Draw some pictures or use objects and ask questions such as the following, using only multiples of 2, 3, 4, 5, or 10.

- If ♥ stands for 4 objects, then ♥♥♥♥ stand for _____ objects.

- If $ stands for $3, then $27 is shown with _____ $'s.

- If 🌲🌲🌲🌲🌲 stands for 25 trees, then one 🌲 stands for _____ trees.

- If ☆ ☆ ☆ ☆ ☆ ☆ represents 60, then 90 can be shown by _____ ☆'s.

 Learning Tasks 2-3, US› pp. 86-87, 3d› pp. 82-83

2. (a) **8**   (b) **24**   (c) **US› Carlos**   (d) **12**   (e) **16**
                                 (c) **3d› Ahmad**

3. (a) **20**   (b) **5**   (c) **Goldfish**   (d) **35**   (e) **$50**   (f) **$3**

 Workbook Exercises 57-58

Review

 ➤ Review all topics

 Review F, US› p. 88, 3d› p. 84

1. (a) **809**   (b) **788**   (c) **841**

2. (a) **203**   (b) **38**   (c) **77**

3. (a) **10**   (b) **24**   (c) **60**

4. (a) **7**   (b) **6**   (c) **3**

5. Weight of pineapple = weight of both – weight of mango
    = 950 g – 380 g = **570 g**

6. Number sold = number made – number left over = 300 – 12 = **288**

7. Amount in each bag = total kg – number of bags = 20 kg ÷ 2 = **10 kg**

8. Total amount = no. of liters each week x no. of weeks = 10 ℓ x 5 = **50 ℓ**

9. (a) number sold on Tuesday = number sold Monday – number fewer
        = 495 – 98 = **397**
    (b) Total sold = number sold on Monday + number sold on Tuesday
        = 495 + 397 = **892**

Review G, US› p. 89, 3d› p. 85

1. (a) **204**   (b) **1000**   (c) **510**

2. (a) **109**   (b) **208**   (c) **48**

3. (a) **18**   (b) **12**   (c) **40**

4. (a) **4**   (b) **4**   (c) **7**

5. Number of pieces = total length ÷ length of each piece = 28 m ÷ 4 m = **7** m

6. Amount needed = total amount – amount it has now = 250 ℓ - 185 ℓ = **65 ℓ**

7. Number left = total number – number given away = 30 – 14 = **16**

8. **5:20 p.m.**

9. Cost of book = total money – money left = $9 - $3.80 **= $5.20**

10. (a) Total oranges = number of oranges in one day x number of days
        = 2 x 5 **= 10**
    (b) Total oranges = Number of oranges in one day x days in a week
        = 2 x 7 **= 14**

Unit 8 – Geometry

Part 1 – Flat and Curved Faces

(1) Faces and Shapes (US> pp. 90-92, 3d> pp. 86-88)

➤ Identify rectangles, circles, squares, and triangles on 3-dimensional objects.
➤ Identify flat and curved faces on 3-dimensional objects.

In *Primary Mathematics 1*, students learned to identify the four basic shapes — squares, rectangles, circles, and triangles — and to combine these shapes into new shapes. Here, your student will learn to recognize these shapes on three dimensional objects and distinguish between flat and curved surfaces.

The shapes used in the text are primarily cubes, cuboids (rectangular prisms), cylinders, cones, and triangular prisms.

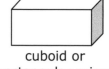

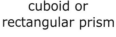

cuboid or
rectangular prism

In this curriculum, rectangular prisms are given the name of cuboid. Your student may use familiar names — such as box, can, or cone — he does not need to identify the 3-dimensional shapes by its geometrical name yet.

triangular prism

Students should handle real objects or 3-dimensional models which contain the four basic shapes.

Review the names of circles, squares, rectangles, and triangles, if necessary.

Use various objects in the shape of cubes, cylinders, triangular prisms, rectangular prisms, or cones. Show your student which faces are flat and which are curved. The flat faces can be placed against paper and traced. Have her identify the traced figures.

Blindfold your student and have her identify the flat faces by feel.

US> pp. 90-91, 3d> pp. 86-87
Learning Task 1, US> p. 92, 3d> p. 88

1. (a) **A**   (b) **C**   (c) **D**   (d) **B**

 Workbook Exercise 59

Part 2 – Making Shapes

(1) Combining Shapes (US› pp. 93-95, 3d› pp. 89-91)

- ➢ Combine common shapes to make new shapes.
- ➢ Identify half circles and quarter circles

Students formed compound figures in *Primary Mathematics 1*. This will be reviewed here and then extended to include half circles and quarter circles.

US› p. 93, 3d› p. 89
Learning Tasks 1-2, US› pp. 94-95, 3d› pp. 90-91

➤ Use a square piece of paper. Fold and then cut along the diagonals. Ask your student to use the 4 triangles to form a rectangle and a larger triangle.

Workbook Exercises 60-61

(2) Curves (US› pp. 96-97, 3d› pp. 92-93)

➢ Divide a shape into common shapes.
➢ Identify straight and curved lines.

 Learning Tasks 3-5, US› pp. 96-97, 3d› pp. 92-93

 Use tangrams, or cut out the ones in the appendix. There are 7 shapes, two large right triangles, one square, two small right triangles, a medium right triangle, and a parallelogram. Have your student combine all seven shapes to create a square unit.

Have yours student use the smaller shapes to cover the large right triangle in different ways.

You can review fractions here. Pointing to each tangram piece in the square formed from each shape; ask your student what fraction of the whole square it is.

Large right triangle: $\frac{1}{4}$

Medium right triangle, square, and parallelogram: $\frac{1}{8}$

Small right triangle: $\frac{1}{16}$

 Workbook Exercises 62-63

(3) Patterns (US› pp. 98-99, 3d› pp. 94-95)

 ➤ Describe and continue a pattern according to one or two attributes of color, shape, size, or orientation.

 In *Primary Mathematics 1*, students learned to recognize and continue patterns based on one or two attributes — size, shape, or color. Here they will also look for patterns based on orientation.

 Learning Tasks 6-7, US› pp. 98-99, 3d› pp. 94-95
In each of these, discuss what attribute is changing. Sometimes it is shape, sometimes pattern, sometimes orientation, sometimes two of these. Your student may find it easier to figure out the pattern by saying it aloud. For example, in 6(a) only shape is changing, and the pattern is "circle, triangle, circle, square, circle, triangle, ..." In 7(e) both size and orientation changes. The student can say "big, little, big, little ..." to determine the next size (big), and then for the large square say "bottom, top, bottom, top..." or "right, left, right, left..." to determine the orientation of the colors for the next image.

6. (a) shape

    (b) size and shape

    (c) size and shape

    (d) orientation

    (e) shape and orientation

7. (a) orientation

    (b) orientation

    (c) shape and orientation

    (d) color and orientation of small circle in triangle (next figure has yellow circle)

    (e) size and orientation; same as third figure.

 Workbook Exercise 64

Review

 ➢ Review all topics

 Review H, US› pp. 100-101, 3d› pp. 99-100

1. (a) **825**   (b) **300**   (c) **541**
2. (a) **160**   (b) **159**   (c) **303**
3. (a) **16**   (b) **70**   (c) **28**
4. (a) **8**   (b) **6**   (c) **10**
5. (a) **$10**   (b) **$1.81**   (c) **$1.50**
6. (a) **18**   (b) **15**   (c) **2**
   (d) **31**   (e) **72**   (f) **83**

7. $\dfrac{2}{5}$

8. $32 \div 4 = 8$ Each circle stands for **8** oranges

9. **8:20 p. m.**

10. 2 50¢ coins for $1, 5 x 2 = 10 for $5   **10** coins

11. Weight of box = 340 g – 100 g = **240 g**

12. Number of children = 275 – 206 = **69**

13. Difference = $8.25 - $6.50 = **$1.75**

14. Total cost = $8 x 5 = **$40**

15. (a) Cost of one chair = $30 ÷ 3 = **$10**
    (b) Cost of table = $120 - $30 = **$90**

16. (a) Number of adults = 168 + 287 = **455**
    (b) Number more adults than children = 455 – 113 = **342**

 Workbook Review 6

Unit 9 – Area

Part 1 – Square Units

(1) Area I (US› pp. 102-104, 3d› pp. 99-100)

> ➢ Understand the concept of area
> ➢ Determine and compare the areas of figures in square units.

The area of a figure is the amount of 2-dimensional space covered by a figure. It is measured in square units. Your student will be measuring and comparing areas in nonstandard square units. The final areas will include only whole or half units at this stage.

Tell your student that area is the amount of flat space covered. Discuss the term in everyday use, such as area rug, area of a room, acres of land, etc.

Use squares. You can copy the page with squares in the back of this guide and cut the squares out, or cut them out of index cards, or use pattern block squares. Tell your student that area is measured in squares. One square has an area of one square unit. If you have a tile floor with squares he can measure the area by counting the number of square tile units. Put several squares together and have him count them to find the area in square units. Cut some of the squares in half diagonally (If you have pattern blocks use the triangle). Ask him for the area of each resulting triangle (half a square unit).

US› page 102, 3d› page 98
Learning Tasks 1-3, US› pp. 103-104, 3d› pp. 99-100

       6

1. (a) **24**   (b) **12**   (c) **22**

2. (a) **7**   (b) **6**   (c) **8**   (d) **C**   (e) **B**

3. **D and F**

Enrichment: Give your student five squares and ask him to find out how many different shapes he can make from them. The side of squares next to each other must touch all along the side. There are 12 unique shapes.

Workbook Exercise 65

(2) Area II (US› p. 105, 3d› p. 101)

 ➤ Measure and compare area in square units.

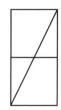

➤ Cut out two squares together and cut them in half as shown here. Ask your student for the area of the resulting triangle. The area of each triangle is one square unit, since if both halves are put together there are two square units.

 Learning Tasks 4-5, US› p 105, 3d› p. 101

4. (a) **6**   (b) **9**

5. P - **7**   Q - **8**   R - **8**   S - **12**

➤ Enrichment:
Draw some other squares and draw an irregular curved shape through them. Shade one part.

Ask your student whether the shaded part is more or less than one half of a square. Tell her two figures, one more than half a square, and less than half a square, can be counted together to have an area of *about* 1 square. Draw an irregular shape on square graph paper and shade it. Have her count the whole squares and write the total down. Then have her pair and mark off squares that are less than half shaded with squares that are more than half shaded. You can tally the number of almost 1 square unit. Then have her give you the total area of the figure as almost _____ square units.

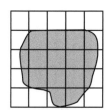

Area is about 13 and a half square units.

Give your student some square graph paper. Have her trace her hand and find the area of his hand prints. She can compare the areas of his hand with the area of another person's hand, or with her foot print.

➤ Enrichment:
Draw 4 squares as shown here:
Ask
    How many squares of 1 square unit
    are there? (4).
    Is there a larger square? (yes)
    What is the area of the larger square? (4 square units.)
    How many total squares does the figure have? (5)

Draw 9 squares in a larger square:
Ask
   How many squares of 1 unit square? (9)
   How many squares of 4 unit squares? (4)
   (They overlap.)
   Is there a larger square? (Yes)
   What is the area of the larger square? (9 square units)
   How many total squares does the figure have? (14)

Draw 16 squares:
Ask
   How many total squares does the figure have? (30)

Help your student determine how many there are of
each size.
There are 16 1-unit squares, 9 4-unit squares, 4 9-unit
squares, and 1 16-unit square.

 Workbook Exercises 66-67

Review

 ➤ Review all topics

 Review I, US› pp. 106-108, 3d› pp. 102-104

1. (a) **500**   (b) **850**   (c) **901**

2. (a) **480**   (b) **603**   (c) **259**

3. (a) **27**   (b) **90**   (c) **30**

4. (a) **7**   (b) **10**   (c) **1**

5. (a) **$10**   (b) **$9.20**   (c) **$1.40**

6. (a) **302**   (b) **101**   (c) **566**   (d) **225**

7. (a) **70**   (b) **200**   (c) **50**   (d) **909**

8. (a) **257, 275, 752**   (b) $\frac{1}{9}, \frac{1}{6}, \frac{1}{3}$

9. Amount of money in 50¢ coins = $2; amount of money in 5¢ coins = $0.15
   Total money = $2 + $0.15 = **$2.15**

10. Distance from finishing point = 100 m – 48 m = **52 m**

11. **10 hrs**

12. A is **17** square units, B is **16** square units, **A** is larger.

13. Total time = 2 hours x 5 = **10 hrs**

14. Number of cans = $16 ÷ $2 = **8**

15. Money needed = $8.60 - $6.80 = **$1.80**

16. Number of girls = 305 – 46 = **259**

17. Amount used this month = 128 ℓ + 25 ℓ = **153 ℓ**

18. Cost of one plate = $24 ÷ 4 = **$6**

19. (a) Cost of oven = $960 - $425 = **$535**
    (b) Total cost = $960 + $535 = **$1,495**

20. (a) Pages read in 6 days = 10 x 6 = **60**
    (b) Total pages = 60 + 24 = **84**

Review J, US› pp. 109-112

1. Length of other piece = 9 in. – 5 in. = **4 in.**

2. Total cost = $3 x 7 = **$21**

3. Number of dresses = 24 ÷ 4 = **6**

4. The pencil is shorter by **1 in.**

5. Number of quarts sold this month = 302 qt + 29 qt = **331 qt.**

6. Amount more gallons needed = 115 gal – 38 gal = **77 gal**

7. Weight of sister = 65 lb – 19 lb = **46 lb**

8. Length of each piece = 18 yd ÷ 3 = **6 yd**

9. 1 ft = **12** in.

10. 1 qt = **4** c

11. **9** lb; **8** oz

12. (a) Number of cups he drinks in 6 days = 2 c x 6 = **12 c**

    (b) Number of cups he drinks in 1 week = 2 c x 7 = **14 c**

13. Cost of 1 lb of shrimp = $45 ÷ 5 = **$9**

14. Total cost = $3 x 9 = **$27**

15. Weight of peach = 15 oz – 8 oz = **7 oz**

16. 1 gal = **4** qt

17. Total length of ribbon needed = 2 yd x 4 = **8 yd**

18. (a) Weight of lettuce = 14 oz – 3 oz = **11 oz**
    (b) Total weight = 14 oz + 11 oz = **25 oz**

19. Length of each piece = 16 ft ÷ 4 = **4 ft**

20. Weight of 10 bags = 2 lb x 10 = **20 lb**

21. Check student's drawing. Line should be 9 in. long.

22. (a) Weight of Emma's mother = 59 lb + 78 lb = **137 lb**
    (b) Total weight = 59 lb + 137 lb = **196 lb**

23. Water in each container = 28 qt ÷ 4 = **7 qt**

24. 1 m is slightly longer than 1 yd. **Yes**, the ribbon is longer.

25. Total cups of milk needed = 2 c x 7 = **14 c**

26. Total length = 18 in. + 31 in. + 25 in. = **74 in.**

27. Total distance = 470 yd + 250 yd = **720 yd**

28. (a) Total weight = 65 lb + 127 lb + 88 lb = **280 lb**
    (b) Difference between John's and David's weight = 127 lb – 65 lb = **62 lb**

29. (a) **7** oz
    (b) Weight of apple = 15 oz – 7 oz = **8** oz
    (c) The **apple** weighs **1** oz more.

Workbook Review 7
Workbook Review 8

Answers and Solutions to Workbook Exercises

Exercise 1

1.   (a) **16**   (b) **12**   (c) **16**

2.   (across, then down) **20**; **70**; **35**; **40**; **45**; **30**; **75**; **100**; **80**   **YOUR TEETH**

Exercise 2

1.   (down, then across) **10**; **40**; **95**; **70**; **2**; **85**

2.   (a) **1**   (b) **5**   (c) **4**   (d) **9**
     (e) **20**   (f) **65**   (g) **16**   (h) **37**
     (i) **58**   (j) **42**   (k) **94**   (l) **91**

3.   **80**; **90**; **60**; **30**

4.   (a) **2**   (b) **7**   (c) **15**   (d) **73**
     (e) **21**   (f) **44**   (g) **78**   (h) **66**
     (i) **91**   (j) **93**   (k) **99**   (l) **96**

Exercise 3

1.   (a) **2**   (b) **60**   (c) **38**
     (d) **40**   (e) **80**   (f) **27**

2.   (a) **27**   (b) **58**   (c) **69**   (d) **48**
     (e) **88**   (f) **79**   (g) **34**   (h) **71**
     (i) **28**   (j) **80**   (k) **40**   (l) **64**
     (m) **51**   (n) **97**   (o) **63**   (p) **54**

3.   (a) **60**   (b) **60**   (c) **90**   (d) **70**
     (e) **120**   (f) **130**   (g) **130**   (h) **130**
     (i) **120**   (j) **150**   (k) **140**   (l) **180**

4.   (a) **45**   (b) **68**   (c) **96**   (d) **87**
     (e) **103**   (f) **109**   (g) **102**   (h) **109**
     (i) **118**   (j) **123**   (k) **107**   (l) **122**

Exercise 4

1.   (a) **166**   (b) **235**   (c) **409**
     (d) **407**   (e) **788**   (f) **659**

2.   (a) **141**   (b) **196**   (c) **362**   (d) **415**
     (e) **572**   (f) **664**   (g) **743**   (h) **298**

3. (a) **260**   (b) **549**   (c) **482**   (d) **658**
    (e) **765**   (f) **375**   (g) **677**   (h) **893**

4. (a) **310**   (b) **500**   (c) **728**   (d) **615**
    (e) **466**   (f) **955**   (g) **845**   (h) **780**

5. (a) **400**   (b) **800**   (c) **900**   (d) **500**
    (e) **800**   (f) **700**   (g) **600**   (h) **900**

6. (a) **450**   (b) **706**   (c) **675**   (d) **909**
    (e) **864**   (f) **525**   (g) **715**   (h) **935**

Exercise 5

1. (a) **70**   (b) **4**   (c) **89**

2. (a) **70; 72** (b) **95; 99**   (c) **72; 75**   (d) **94; 99**

3. (a) **57**   (b) **66**   (c) **87**
    (d) **48**   (e) **89**   (f) **99**

Exercise 6

1. **101   102   105**
    101   104   105

2. (a) **136**   (b) **152**   (c) **144**   (d) **163**

Exercise 7

1. (a) **282**   (b) **344**   (c) **298**   (d) **304**
    (e) **655**   (f) **333**   (g) **507**   (h) **497**

Exercise 8

1. (a) **15**   (b) **10**   (c) **71**
    (d) **13**   (e) **50**   (f) **32**

2. (a) **21**   (b) **64**   (c) **31**   (d) **51**
    (e) **72**   (f) **91**   (g) **18**   (h) **58**
    (i) **78**   (j) **46**   (k) **39**   (l) **66**
    (m) **46**   (n) **28**   (o) **95**   (p) **78**

3. (a) **18**   (b) **56**   (c) **65**   (d) **43**
    (e) **22**   (f) **34**   (g) **71**   (h) **87**

4. (a) **10**   (b) **20**   (c) **30**   (d) **40**
    (e) **10**   (f) **10**   (g) **0**   (h) **10**

5. (a) **21**   (b) **33**   (c) **27**   (d) **18**
    (e) **14**   (f) **25**   (g) **59**   (h) **12**

Exercise 9

1. (a) **872**   (b) **934**   (c) **412**   (d) **262**   (e) **103**   (f) **653**
2. (a) **442**   (b) **678**   (c) **888**   (d) **556**
    (e) **228**   (f) **944**   (g) **718**   (h) **137**
3. (a) **503**   (b) **757**   (c) **121**   (d) **327**
    (e) **230**   (f) **806**   (g) **632**   (h) **428**
4. (a) **469**   (b) **658**   (c) **186**   (d) **283**
    (e) **377**   (f) **545**   (g) **198**   (h) **771**
5. (a) **100**   (b) **200**   (c) **700**   (d) **200**
    (e) **400**   (f) **300**   (g) **100**   (h) **300**
6. (a) **433**   (b) **89**   (c) **153**   (d) **394**
    (e) **235**   (f) **227**   (g) **286**   (h) **168**

Exercise 10

1. (a) **2**   (b) **80**   (c) **52**
2. (a) **48;43**   (b) **25;21**   (c) **14;11**   (d) **28; 22**
3. (a) **42**   (b) **12**   (c) **23**   (d) **14**   (e) **21**   (f) **25**
4. (clockwise from top) **89; 55; 58; 98**
5. (a) **23**   (b) **89**   (c) **74**   (d) **40**   (e) **22**   (f) **89**

Exercise 11

1. (a) **201**   (b) **401**   (c) **601**   (d) **701**
    (e) **302**   (f) **502**   (g) **202**   (h) **802**

Exercise 12

1. (a) **81**   (b) **203**   (c) **457**   (d) **749**
    (e) **107**   (f) **369**   (g) **682**   (h) **534**

Review 1

1. **769; 405; 30; 60**
2. (a) **350**   (b) **704**
3. **90; 56; 500; 680**
    55; 93; 32; 100

4. $879 \rightarrow 889 \rightarrow 897 \rightarrow 978 \rightarrow 987 \rightarrow 990$

5.
seashells: 99	shells given: 26
total shells: ?	

Total seashells = seashells + shells given by friend
     = 99 + 26 = **125**

6.
starting money: $300	
money spent: ?	money left: $98

Money spent = money she started with – money left
     = $300 - $98 = **$202**

7.
US› Sara's, **3d**› Suhua's stickers: 135	amount more: 45
US› Emily's, **3d**› Meilin's stickers: ?	

US› Emily's stickers = Sara's stickers + amount more
US› Meilin's stickers = Suhua's stickers + amount more
     = 135 + 45 = **180**

8.
saved both months: $200	
saved in January: ?	saved in February: $85

Amount saved in January = total amount – amount saved in February
     = $200 - $85 = **$115**

9.
weight of papaya: 650 g	
weight of mango: ?	difference: 200 g

Weight of mango = weight of papaya – difference
     = 650 g – 200 g = **450 g**

10. Total distance = distance he has walked + distance left
     = 350 m + 250 m = **600 m**

Exercise 13

1.   **4, 8, 12, 16, 20, 24, 28, 32, 36, 40**

2.   (a) **4**   (b) **8**   (c) **12**   (d) **16**   (e) **20**
     (f) **24**   (g) **28**   (h) **32**   (i) **36**   (j) **40**

Exercise 14

1.   (a) **8; 8**   (b) **12; 12**   (c) **28; 28**   (d) **36, 36**

Exercise 15

1. (a) **12**   (b) **24**   (c) **20**   (d) **40**

2. **16**; **32**; **28**; **36**; **20**; **28**

Exercise 16

1. left side: 2 x 4 → 8; 3 x 4 → 12; 6 x 4 → 24; 8 x 4 → 32
    right side: 9 x 4 → 36; 7 x 4 → 28; 5 x 4 → 20; 10 x 4 → 40

2.

row 5 trees	row 5 trees	row 5 trees	row 5 trees
total trees: ?			

Total trees = number of rows x number of trees in each row = 4 x 5 = **20**

3.

side 6 cm	side 6 cm	side 6 cm	side 6 cm
total length: ?			

Total length = number of sides x length of each side = 4 x 6 = **24 cm**

4. Total fish = number of boys x number of fish each boy caught = 4 x 3 = **12**

Exercise 17

1. **8**; **14**; **15**; **21**; **18**; **20**; **32**; **18**; **24**; **10**; **40**; **9**; **36**; **24**

2.

shirt $4	shirt $4	shirt $4	shirt $4	shirt $4	shirt $4
total length: ?					

Total cost = number of shirts x cost of each shirt = 6 x 4 = **24**

2.

cloth 3 m	cloth 3 m	cloth 3 m	cloth 3 m	cloth 3 m	cloth 3 m	cloth 3 m	cloth 3 m	cloth 3 m
total length: ?								

Total length = number of pieces of cloth x length of each piece = 9 x 3 = **27 m**

3. Total kg of cooking oil = number of bottles x kg in each bottle = 10 x 2 = **20 kg**

Exercise 18

1. **1**   **2**
    3   **4, 4**
    5, 5   **6, 6**
    10, 10   **7, 7**
    9, 9   **8, 8**

2. clockwise from top: $32 \div 4 \ \square\ 8$; $20 \div 4 \ \square\ 5$; $36 \div 4 \ \square\ 9$; $8 \div 4 \ \square\ 2$;
    $12 \div 4 \ \square\ 3$; $28 \div 4 \ \square\ 7$; $16 \div 4 \ \square\ 4$; $24 \div 4 \ \square\ 6$

3. We are given the total number of children, 36. There are 4 equal parts, or
    rows. We need to find how many are in each part. We divide.
    $36 \div 4 = 9$
    There are **9** children in each row.

4. We are given the total cost, $24, and the number of equal parts, 4 kg. We
    need to find how much money is in each part, or 1 kg. We divide.
    $24 \div 4 = 6$
    Each kg cost **$6**.

5. We are given the total length, 28 m, and the number of equal parts, 4. We
    need to find how many meters are in each part. We divide.
    $28 \div 4 = 7$
    Each piece is **7 m** long.

Exercise 19

1. **5; 10; 15; 20; 25; 30; 35; 40; 45; 50**

Exercise 20

1. left side: $7 \times 5 \rightarrow 35$; $5 \times 3 \rightarrow 15$; $8 \times 5 \rightarrow 40$; $5 \times 6 \rightarrow 30$; $2 \times 5 \rightarrow 10$
    right side: $4 \times 5 \rightarrow 20$; $10 \times 5 \rightarrow 50$; $5 \times 9 \rightarrow 45$; $1 \times 5 \rightarrow 5$; $5 \times 5 \rightarrow 25$

2. Total cakes = number of boxes x 6 cakes in each box = $5 \times 6 =$ **30**

3. Total packets = number of pots x number of packets for each pot = $3 \times 5 =$ **15**

4. Total spent = number of weeks x amount spent each week = $4 \times \$10 =$ **$40**

Exercise 21

1. **1**   **2**
    3   **7, 7**
    5, 5   **9, 9**
    4, 4   **6, 6**
    8, 8   **10, 10**

2. clockwise from pole: $8 \to 40 \div 5$; $7 \to 35 \div 5$; $9 \to 45 \div 5$; $4 \to 20 \div 5$;
    $10 \to 50 \div 5$; $5 \to 25 \div 5$; $3 \to 15 \div 5$; $6 \to 30 \div 5$

3. Pencils in each bundle = total pencils ÷ number of bundles = $40 \div 5$ = **8**

4. Number of weeks = total money ÷ amount saved each week = $50 \div $5 = **10**

5. Amount for each student = total money ÷ number of students = $20 \div 5 = **$4**

Exercise 22

1. **10**; **20**; **30**; **40**; **50**; **60**; **70**; **80**; **90**; **100**

2. **50**; **20**; **40**
      30; **32**
   40; **20**; **12**
      35; **50**

3. Soldiers in 10 rows = soldiers in 1 row x number of rows = 5×10 = **50**

4. 1 dictionary cost $10
   10 dictionaries cost 10×10 = **$100**

5. Total = cost of 1 m x number of meters = 7×10 = **$70**

Exercise 23

1.   **3**   **3**   **3**
     5   5   **8   8**
     6   6   **4   4**
     7   7   **2   2**
     1   1   **9   9**

2. $10 = 100 \div 10$; $7 = 70 \div 10$; $2 = 20 \div 10$; $9 = 90 \div 10$;
   $5 = 50 \div 10$; $8 = 80 \div 10$; $6 = 60 \div 10$; $4 = 40 \div 10$

3. $60 \div 10 = 6$ One bag weighs **6 kg**.

4. $40 \div 10 = 4$ One plant costs **$4**.

5. $90 \div 10 = 9$ There were **9** chairs in each row.

Review 2

1. (a) **336**   (b) **84**   (c) **584**   (d) **206**   (e) **798**   (f) **302**

2. (a) **44**; **300**;   (b) **22**; **40**;
       344   **62**
          344   **62**

3.   (A) **12**; **14**; **5**; **8**   (B) **27**; **12**; **6**; **8**(C)   **32**; **24**; **5**; **7**
     (D) **25**; **45**; **6**; **8**   (E) **30**; **50**; **6**; **9**
     (F) **30**; **10**; **10**; **10**   (G) **18**; **9**; **7**; **9**

4.   Number of tickets sold 2nd day = total sold – number sold first day
                               = 402 – 382 = **20**

5.   Total pencils = number of boxes x number of pencils in each box
                  = 3 x 10 = **30**

6.   Number of boats = total people ÷ number of people in a boat
                  = 40 ÷ 5 = **8**

7.   1 kg cost $5   9 kg cost $5 x 9 = **$45**

8.   Envelopes needed = total letters – envelopes already had
                     = 122 – 86 = **36**

9.   Total people = number of boys + number of girls + number of adults
                 = 386 + 255 + 145 = **786**

Exercise 24

1.   **$0.95**; **$0.59**; **$1.65**; **$1.56**; **$2.25**

2.   (a) **$0.92**   (b) **$3.20**   (c) **$5.85**   (d) **$6.04**   (e) **$18.05**

3.   (a) **$0.84**   (b) **$24.00** (c) **$58.40** (d) **$58.55**

Exercise 25

1.   left side: 5 dollars 45 cents; 5 dollars 50 cents; 4 dollars 40 cents; 85 cents;
     right side: 9 dollars 60 cents; 8 dollars; 6 dollars 90 cents; 4 dollars 5 cents

2.   **$3.05**; **$4.30**; **$5.00**; **$0.50**; **$9.75**; **$9.90**

3.   **6, 80**   **4, 65**   **0, 70**   **6, 45**   **7, 0**

Exercise 26

1. $23.00 $4.00 $13.30 $0.20 $7.50 $99.05

2.   **$0.15**   **$20.00**   **$47.00**   **$74.50**   **$30.45**
     $86.05   **$47.15**   **$0.95**   **$95.05**   **$40.25**

Exercise 27

1.   180¢   270¢   345¢   105¢
     $0.10 $0.05 $0.35 $3.00

2.   (down) **$1.00**; **$2.00**; **$1.25**; **$2.40**; **$3.60**; **$4.05**
      $2.05; **$1.90**; **$3.50**; **$0.85**; **$0.70**; **$0.05**

3.   (down) **$0.30**; **$0.45**; **$1.20**; **$2.50**; **$3.00**; **$0.75**; **$3.45**, **$0.06**
      10¢; **75¢**; **105¢**; **305¢**; **250¢**; **150¢**; **400¢**; **8¢**

Exercise 28

1.   (a) **55¢**   (b) **5¢**   (c) **25¢**   (d) **65¢**

2.   (clockwise from lower left) **15¢**; **25¢**; **20¢**; **30¢**; **35¢**; **45¢**

Exercise 29

1.   (a) **$0.80**   (b) **$1.60**   (c) **$7.40**   (d) **$6.90**

2.   (a) **50; 3.00; 3.50**   (b) **85, 7.00, 7.85**   (c) **5.30**

Exercise 30

1.   Change = $1 – 45¢ = **55¢**

2.   Money left = $10 - $5.20 = **$4.80**

3.   (a) 55¢ + 45¢ = **$1.00**
      (b) $1 – 85¢ = **15¢**
      (c) $10 - $8.20 = **$1.80**
      (d) $10 - $4.40 = **$5.60**
      (e) table-tennis racket and flying saucer

Exercise 31

1.   (a) **4.85**   (b) **4.45**   (c) **10.05**   (d) **13.70**
      (e) **2.55**   (f) **1.90**   (g) **2.75**   (h) **3.80**
      (i) **4.00**   (j) **3.00**   (k) **5.00**   (l) **5.00**

Exercise 32

1.   (a) **3.45; 3.75; 3.75**
      (b) **5.60; 5.85; 5.85**
      (c) **5.15; 5.80; 5.80**

2.   (a) **$3.60**   (b) **$6.90**   (c) **$4.90**
      (d) **$4.80**   (e) **$5.60**   (f) **$8.90**

Exercise 33

1. E **$3.05**   F **$5.45**   L **$3.55**
    N **$8.35**   O **$8.10**   R **$9.20**
    S **$6.20**   U **$6.00**   W **$9.10**
    SUNFLOWER

Exercise 34

1. (a) **$3.44**   (b) **$8.14**   (c) **$5.54**   (d) **$6.24**
2. (a) **$4.75**   (b) **$3.60**   (c) **$6.35**   (d) **$8.30**

Exercise 35

1. (a) **1.85**   (b) **4.45**   (c) **3.05**   (d) **1.25**
    (e) **2.35**   (f) **5.05**   (g) **6.00**   (h) **9.15**
    (i) **3.20**   (j) **4.30**   (k) **2.45**   (l) **5.25**

Exercise 36

1. (a) **4.80; 4.30; 4.30**   (b) **1.75; 1.40; 1.40**
    (c) **2.90; 2.25; 2.25**
2. (a) **$3.60**   (b) **$3.25**   (c) **$2.15**
    (d) **$4.35**   (e) **$2.45**   (f) **$4.25**

Exercise 37

1. A **$1.65**   D **$2.55**   F **$4.75**
    G **$2.30**   L **$2.85**   N **$4.60**
    O **$2.60**   R **$0.45**   Y **$1.55**
    DRAGONFLY

Exercise 38

1. (a) **$3.31**   (b) **$2.46**   (c) **$2.26**   (d) **$3.01**
2. (a) **$1.25**   (b) **$2.60**   (c) **$0.15**   (d) **$2.30**

Workbook Exercise 39

1. Total money = cost of ball + cost of airplane = $2.40 + $3.25 = **$5.65**

2. Money left = money he started with – cost of toy car = $8 - $5.35 = **$2.65**

3.
cost of robot: $5.90	
cost of doll: $3.85	?

    ? = $5.90 - $3.85 = **$2.05**

4. Cost of stamps = $2 + 75¢ + 20¢ = $2.95
    Money she started with = cost of stamps + money she had left
    $\qquad\qquad$ = $2.95 + $6.30 = **$9.25**

5. Amount his brother spent = amount he spent + amount more
    $\qquad\qquad$ = $2.60 + $0.95 = **$3.55**

6.
Lily's savings: $10	
Alice's savings: ?	$1.95

    Alice's savings = $10 - $1.95 = **$8.05**

Review 3

1. (a) **451**   (b) **960**

2. (a) **999**   (b) **700**   (c) **908**

3. (a) **m**   (b) **cm**   (c) **cm**   (d) **m**

4. (a) **kg**   (b) **g**   (c) **g**   (d) **kg**

5. (a) **1000**   (b) **264**
    (c) **$5.90**   (d) **$2.80**
    (e) **$5.54**   (f) **$7.05**

6. (a) **7; 7**   (b) **8; 8**   (c) **9; 9**   (d) **8; 8**

7. Total pens = number of packets x number of pens in each packet = 8 x 3 = **24**

8. Length of a piece = total length ÷ number of pieces = 20 m ÷ 5 = **4 m**

9. Change received = cash given – cost of book = $10 - $5.35 = **$4.65**

10. Weight of papaya = 920 g – 135 g = **785 g**

11. Kg of meat needed = 6 kg x 4 = **24 kg**

12. Cost of pen = $9.50 - $1.60 = **$7.90**

Review 4

1. (a) **6; 9; 18; 24**   (b) **20; 32; 36; 40**
    (c) **15; 20; 30; 35**   (d) **30; 40; 50; 70; 90**

2. (a) **405**; **413** (b) **596**; **600** (c) **402**; **398** (d) **866**; **858**

3. (a) **506**   (b) **707**   (c) **802**   (d) **394**

4. (a) **$0.40**   (b) **$0.80**   (c) **$0.55**   (d) **$2.15**

5. Bag A: $7.05   Bag B: $4.50
    $7.05 - $4.50 = $2.55
    There is **$2.55** more in bag A than in bag B.

6. Amount each paid = $36 ÷ 4 = **$9**

7. Total amount paid = 6 x $4 = **$24**

8. Number of packets = 45 ÷ 5 = **9**

9. More mangoes = 28 – 19 = **9**

10. Number of words he learns in 5 weeks = 7 x 5 = **35**

11. Number of books in library at first = 26 + 34 = **60**

Exercise 40

1. First and second one of first row; first and third one of second row.

2. First one of first row; first, second and fourth one of second row.

5. (b) **>**

Exercise 41

1. (a) $\dfrac{2}{3}$ (b) $\dfrac{5}{8}$ (c) $\dfrac{7}{10}$ (d) $\dfrac{3}{4}$

2. (a) **1, 6**   (b) **2, 5**   (c) **1, 3**   (d) **3, 4**   (e) **5, 8**

Exercise 42

1. The fraction is straight across from the picture for each.

2. The lines form a cross-hatched picture with the fish in the middle of each diamond shape.

3. A $\dfrac{3}{4}$ C $\dfrac{2}{3}$ F $\dfrac{3}{5}$

    I $\dfrac{5}{6}$ O $\dfrac{1}{6}$ N $\dfrac{2}{5}$

    R $\dfrac{1}{2}$ S $\dfrac{5}{12}$ T $\dfrac{3}{8}$ FRACTIONS

Exercise 43

Check the fractions colored.

Exercise 44

2. (a) >   (b) <   (c) <   (d) >   (e) <   (f) >

3. (a) $\frac{1}{2}$ (b) $\frac{1}{4}$ (c) $\frac{1}{9}$ (d) $\frac{1}{2}$ (e) $\frac{1}{8}$ (f) $\frac{1}{4}$

4. (a) $\frac{1}{6}$ (b) $\frac{1}{10}$ (c) $\frac{1}{5}$ (d) $\frac{1}{12}$ (e) $\frac{1}{10}$ (f) $\frac{1}{9}$

5. (a) $\frac{1}{2}$ (b) $\frac{1}{5}$ (c) $\frac{1}{4}$ (d) $\frac{1}{5}$

6. (a) $\frac{1}{7}$ (b) $\frac{1}{12}$ (c) $\frac{1}{4}$ (d) $\frac{1}{9}$

7. $\frac{1}{10}$, $\frac{1}{8}$, $\frac{1}{4}$, $\frac{1}{2}$

8. $\frac{1}{3}$, $\frac{1}{5}$, $\frac{1}{9}$, $\frac{1}{12}$

Exercise 45

1. (a) $\frac{2}{3}$ (b) $\frac{6}{8}$ (c) $\frac{3}{5}$ (d) $\frac{5}{6}$

2. clockwise from left: $\frac{1}{3}$; $\frac{5}{8}$; $\frac{1}{6}$; $\frac{1}{4}$; $\frac{2}{5}$; $\frac{1}{2}$

Exercise 46

1. clockwise from top: **0; 5; 10; 15; 20; 25; 30; 35; 40; 45; 50; 55; 50**
    2:50

2. (b) **5; 4:00; 4:15**   (c) **35; 10:00; 10:35**

3. left side: 3:25; 6:00; 2:20; 12:30
    right side: 12:35; 8:55; 9:05; 11:00

4. **7:30**   **8:15**   **1:30**
    5:05   **11:40**   **9:10**
    1:20   **8:50**   **12:45**
    4:25   **6:40**   **9:50**

Exercise 47

1. (a) **5; 3; 5; 3**   (b) **25; 12; 25; 12**
   (c) **20; 3; 20; 3**   (d) **10; 5; 10; 5**

2. (a) **10; 6**   (b) **15; 7**   (c) **15; 7**   (d) **25; 8**

3.

Exercise 48

1. (a) **20**   (b) **15**   (c) **25**   (d) **40**

2. (a) **1**   (b) **4**   (c) **3**   (d) **4**

3. (a) **15**   (b) **35**   (c) **35**   (d) **50**

4. (a) **4:05; 5; 4:10** (b)   **2:50; 10; 3:00**
   (c) **9:30; 40; 10:10**   (d) **5:45; 7; 12:45**

Exercise 49

1. (a) **4:35 a.m.**   (b) **11:50 p.m.**   (c) **6:15 a.m.**
   (d) **6:00 p.m.**   (e) **3:15 a.m.**

2. (a) **5:25 p.m.**   (b) **4:15 a.m.**   (c) **1:40 p.m.**
   (d) **12:10 a.m.**   (e) **2:55 a.m.**

Review 5

1. (a) **569**   (b) **700**   (c) **444**   (d) **300**

2. (a) **40**   (b) **16**   (c) **826**   (d) **704**

3. clockwise from top: **200; 35; 7; 70; 160**. Middle: **63**

4. (a) **$9.00**   (b) **$6.40**   (c) **$3.35**   (d) **$3.10**

5. (a) **<**   (b) **>**   (c) **=**   (d) **>**

6. (a) **36**   (b) **9**   (c) **40**   (d) **8**

7. **2**

8.   (a) Total spent = $6.80 + $5.60 = **$12.40**
      (b) Total money = money spent + money left = $12.40 + $15 = **$27.40**

9.   Total chairs = number of chairs for each table x number of tables
                = 5 x 9 = **45**

10.   Number of children = number of books ÷ number of books each borrowed
                = 20 ÷ 4 = **5**

11.   Total joggers = teachers + boys + girls = 38 + 298 + 162 = **498**

Exercise 50

Check answers.

Exercise 51

1.   **A; B**   2.   **A; B**
3.   **B**   4.   **X**
5.   (a) **B; A**   (b) **2; 2**

Exercise 52

Check answers.

US› Exercise 53

1.   (a) **4**   (b) **4**
2.   (c) **3**   (b) **3**
3.   Amount more = 600 ℓ – 458 ℓ = **142** ℓ
4.   Total amount bought = 5 x 4 ℓ = **20** ℓ

3d› Exercise 53

1.   (a) **4**   (b) **4**
2.   (a) **3**   (b) **3**
3.   (a) **7**   (b) **7**
4.   (a) **5**   (b) **5**

US› Exercise 54

1. Amount needed = 250 gal – 105 gal = **145 gal**
2. Number of quarts in each jug = 16 qt ÷ 8 qt = **2 qt**
3. (a) **7**   (b) **7**
4. (a) **5**   (b) **5**

3d› Exercise 54

1. Amount more = 600 ℓ – 458 ℓ = **142 ℓ**
2. Liters needed = 250 ℓ – 105 ℓ = **145 ℓ**
3. Total amount bought = 5 x 4 ℓ = **20 ℓ**
4. Number of liters in each jug = 16 ℓ ÷ 8= **2 ℓ**

Exercise 55

1. (a) **3**   (b) **6**   (c) **2**   (d) **Red**   (e) **Yellow**
2. (a) **8**   (b) **5**   (c) **5**   (d) **3**   (e) **US› Cameron**
                                                                              (e) **3d› Chengfa**

Exercise 56

1. (a) **10**   (b) **14**   (c) **4**   (d) **6**   (e) **6**

2.

		⬤	
	⬤	⬤	
	⬤	⬤	
	⬤	⬤	⬤
⬤	⬤	⬤	⬤
⬤	⬤	⬤	⬤
Devi	Sally	Weilin	Rosni

Exercise 57

1. (a) **10**   (b) **30**   (c) **12**
2. (a) color **5** squares   (b) color **6** triangles
3. (a) **$9**   (b) **June**   (c) **May**   (d) **$9**   (e) **$30**

Exercise 58

1. (a) **50**   (b) **US› Matthew**   (c) **US› Annie**   (d) **10**   (e) **30**   (f) **70**
                 (b) **3d› Minghua**   (c) **3d› Aihua**
2. (a) **no**   (b) **yes**   (c) **no**   (d) **yes**   (d) **no**

Exercise 59

2. (a) the box   (b) the calendar
3. (a) **rectangle** (b) **circle**   (c) **square**
    (d) **triangle**   (e) **rectangle** (f) **rectangle**
4. (a) A   **1   1**
        B   **5   0**
        C   **6   0**
        D   **2   1**
        E   **6   0**

    (b) **2**   (c) **2**   (d) **2**

Exercise 60

1. first → third   second → fourth   third → second   fourth → first
2. first → second   second → fourth   third → first   fourth → third

---

Exercise 61

1. Answers can vary
    (b)   (c)   (d)

Exercise 62

1. (a) half circle, triangle   (b) triangle, square
    (c) half circle, quarter circle (d) square, rectangle
    (e) quarter circle, rectangle

2.   Answers can vary.

(b)    (c)   (d)   (e)

Exercise 63

Check answers

Exercise 64

1.   (a)   (b)   (c)   (d)

2.   (a)   (b)   (c)   (d)   (e)

Review 6

1.   **18   40   36   90**
     9   8   8   10

2.   (a) **five dollars and ninety cents**
     (b) **nine dollars and fifty cents**
     (c) **five dollars and nine cents**
     (d) **nine dollars and five cents**

3. $\dfrac{2}{3}$, $\dfrac{3}{4}$, $\dfrac{5}{6}$

4.   (a) **5**   (b) **3**

5.   (a) **10**   (b) **30**

US› 6.   money in quarters = $2; money in dimes = $1.20
             Total money = **$3.20**
3d› 6.   money in 50 cent coins = $2; money in 20 cent coins = $1.20
             Total money = **$3.20**

7.   Amount of change = $10 - $3.95 = **$6.05**

8.   Cost of 1 ticket = $35 ÷ 5 = **$7**

9.   Number of pages read on second day = 210 – 145 = **65**

10. Amount saved in 6 weeks = $4 x 6 = **$24.00**

11. Amount sister saved = $245 + $65 = **$310.00**

Exercise 65

1. (a) same   (b) different   (c) same   (d) same   (e) same
2. (a) first   (b) first   (c) first   (d) second   (e) first

---

Exercise 66

1. second to first, third to fifth, fourth to third, fifth to fourth
2. (a) **8**   (b) **5**   (c) **7**   (d) **11**   (e) **9**   (f) **16**

Exercise 67

2. (a) A: **6**   B: **5**   C: **6** D: **7**
    (b) **D**   (c) **B**   (d) **A, C**

Review 7

1. (a) **408**   (b) **250**
2. (a) **950**   (b) **728**   (c) **972**   (d) **620**   (e) **590**
3. (a) **59**   (b) **42**   (c) **37**   (d) **76**
4. (a) **150**   (b) **300**   (c) **500**   (d) **841**
    (e) **396**   (f) **549**   (g) **625**   (h) **73**
5. (a) **=**   (b) **<**
6. (a)   (b)

7. first group: A, F, J, H   second group: C, I, E   third group: B, D, G
8. (a) Number of girls = 120 + 85 = **205**
    (b) Total number of children = 120 + 205 = **325**
    (c) Number of children who wear glasses = 19 + 16 = 35
        Number of children without glasses = 325 – 35 = **290**
9. Total score = 89 + 91 + 90 = **270**
10. Number of picture cards for each boy = 24 ÷ 3 = **8**
11. Total length = 9 x 5 m = **45 m**
12. Money needed = $8.50 - $6.80 = **$1.70**

13. Total liters = 6 ℓ x 10 = **60 ℓ**

14. Number of boxes = 32 ÷ 4 = **8**

Review 8

1. (a) **8, 10, 12, 14, 16, 18, 20**
    (b) **12, 15, 18, 21, 24, 27, 30**
    (c) **16, 20, 24, 28, 32, 36, 40**
    (d) **20, 25, 30, 35, 40, 45, 50**
    (e) **40, 50, 60, 70, 80, 90, 100**

2. (a) ℓ (b) **min** (c) **m** (d) **g**

    (e) **kg** (f) **h** (g) **cm** (h) **ℓ**

4. (a) **6** (b) **5** (c) **A, B**

5. (a) **half circle, triangle** (b) **rectangle, square**

6. (a) **58, 340, 403, 900** (b) $\frac{1}{12}, \frac{1}{7}, \frac{1}{4}, \frac{1}{2}$

7. (a) **20** (b) **5** (c) **30**

8. Difference = 405 – 240 = **165**

9. Cost of one doll = $70 ÷ 10 = **$7**

10. Cost of apples = 20 ÷ 4 = **$5**

11. Number of (**US**> sugar, **3d**> peanut) cookies = 153 – 89 = **64**

12. Amount sister saved = $10.40 - $3.95 = **$6.45**

13. Capacity = 8 x 4 ℓ = **32 ℓ**

14. Amount cheaper = $8.20 - $6.90 = **$1.30**

US> 15. More gallons needed = 50 gal – 38 gal = **12 gal**
3d> 15. More liters needed = 50 ℓ - 38 ℓ = **12 ℓ**

16. Cost of notebook = $5.20 - $1.80 = **$3.40**

US> 17. Weight of one bag = 40 lb ÷ 5 = **8** lb

US> 18. Capacity of tank = 17 gal + 25 gal = **42** gal

US> 19. Cost of book = $3.80 = $0.75 = **$4.30**

US> 20. 24 quarters = 24 ÷ 4 dollars = $6
    Amount of money Ryan has = $6.10. **Yes**

US> 21. Change = 50¢ - 29¢ = **21¢**

US> 22. Total money = $8 + $1.20 + $0.30 = $0.03 = **$9.53**

Answers to Mental Math

Mental Math 1			
1.	75	15.	63
2.	50	16.	24
3.	25	17.	49
4.	1	18.	60
5.	95	19.	10
6.	40	20.	45
7.	62	21.	93
8.	55	22.	67
9.	56	23.	20
10.	90	24.	59
11.	13	25.	18
12.	78	26.	43
13.	96	27.	82
14.	31	28.	29
12, 20, 28, 36			

Mental Math 2			
1.	5	15.	35
2.	30	16.	75
3.	15	17.	70
4.	87	18.	92
5.	65	19.	50
6.	80	20.	85
7.	82	21.	28
8.	23	22.	54
9.	97	23.	25
10.	71	24.	69
11.	34	25.	194
12.	2	26.	127
13.	12	27.	19
14.	16	28.	28
12, 16, 20, 24, 28, 32, 36, 40			

Mental Math 3			
1.	31	15.	92
2.	77	16.	66
3.	71	17.	40
4.	64	18.	82
5.	73	19.	34
6.	31	20.	44
7.	73	21.	27
8.	85	22.	81
9.	80	23.	30
10.	43	24.	78
11.	62	25.	40
12.	40	26.	62
13.	65	27.	91
14.	48	28.	100
15, 25, 30, 40, 45, 50			

Mental Math 4			
1.	98	15.	137
2.	62	16.	130
3.	88	17.	150
4.	82	18.	115
5.	108	19.	146
6.	92	20.	114
7.	144	21.	158
8.	106	22.	113
9.	82	23.	140
10.	112	24.	130
11.	147	25.	122
12.	122	26.	130
13.	120	27.	148
14.	168	28.	134
15, 20, 25. 30, 35, 40, 45, 50			

Mental Math 5			
1.	436	15.	623
2.	220	16.	533
3.	728	17.	865
4.	912	18.	150
5.	116	19.	497
6.	310	20.	311
7.	513	21.	225
8.	760	22.	629
9.	850	23.	544
10.	291	24.	883
11.	854	25.	210
12.	262	26.	323
13.	192	27.	130
14.	995	28.	393
36, 28, 24, 16, 12			

Mental Math 6			
1.	694	15.	335
2.	268	16.	931
3.	220	17.	557
4.	982	18.	216
5.	692	19.	349
6.	146	20.	810
7.	581	21.	752
8.	289	22.	411
9.	420	23.	940
10.	512	24.	332
11.	848	25.	721
12.	325	26.	333
13.	424	27.	247
14.	660	28.	533
40, 35, 30, 25, 20, 15, 10, 5			

Mental Math 7			
1.	96	16.	297
2.	87	17.	476
3.	97	18.	168
4.	98	19.	200
5.	98	20.	989
6.	87	21.	678
7.	76	22.	908
8.	99	23.	832
9.	99	24.	948
10.	98	25.	605
11.	98	26.	536
12.	40	27.	958
13.	89	28.	712
14.	67	29.	811
15.	93	30.	926

Mental Math 8			
1.	123	16.	515
2.	123	17.	332
3.	103	18.	466
4.	131	19.	336
5.	166	20.	701
6.	123	21.	580
7.	140	22.	280
8.	169	23.	423
9.	161	24.	789
10.	143	25.	403
11.	196	26.	224
12.	424	27.	511
13.	315	28.	824
14.	739	29.	293
15.	911	30.	727

Mental Math 9			
1.	137	16.	213
2.	60	17.	235
3.	75	18.	562
4.	121	19.	112
5.	850	20.	100
6.	143	21.	256
7.	728	22.	530
8.	100	23.	445
9.	357	24.	801
10.	198	25.	296
11.	68	26.	100
12.	670	27.	104
13.	379	28.	299
14.	407	29.	161
15.	985	30.	892

Mental Math 10			
1.	82	16.	35
2.	26	17.	75
3.	15	18.	24
4.	66	19.	88
5.	78	20.	58
6.	19	21.	65
7.	56	22.	47
8.	58	23.	47
9.	44	24.	14
10.	87	25.	77
11.	39	26.	36
12.	23	27.	29
13.	46	28.	63
14.	67	29.	39
15.	79	30.	39

Mental Math 11			
1.	282	16.	35
2.	526	17.	875
3.	115	18.	384
4.	966	19.	918
5.	818	20.	638
6.	419	21.	705
7.	646	22.	547
8.	358	23.	947
9.	744	24.	814
10.	367	25.	857
11.	239	26.	416
12.	473	27.	424
13.	546	28.	263
14.	167	29.	412
15.	658	30.	200

Mental Math 12			
1.	268	16.	460
2.	821	17.	150
3.	601	18.	330
4.	358	19.	640
5.	762	20.	460
6.	560	21.	580
7.	730	22.	62
8.	160	23.	477
9.	660	24.	420
10.	330	25.	730
11.	550	26.	33
12.	870	27.	232
13.	420	28.	516
14.	340	29.	42
15.	190	30.	190

Mental Math 13			
1.	79	16.	21
2.	24	17.	35
3.	42	18.	24
4.	45	19.	13
5.	33	20.	64
6.	16	21.	42
7.	13	22.	7
8.	3	23.	22
9.	22	24.	32
10.	31	25.	30
11.	33	26.	32
12.	22	27.	24
13.	37	28.	20
14.	61	29.	31
15.	41	30.	62

Mental Math 14			
1.	101	16.	266
2.	302	17.	687
3.	501	18.	157
4.	401	19.	160
5.	2	20.	664
6.	701	21.	266
7.	262	22.	159
8.	632	23.	105
9.	812	24.	461
10.	521	25.	603
11.	333	26.	486
12.	600	27.	688
13.	744	28.	665
14.	153	29.	115
15.	334	30.	82

Mental Math 15			
1.	25	16.	48
2.	77	17.	180
3.	485	18.	54
4.	63	19.	18
5.	573	20.	588
6.	190	21.	404
7.	586	22.	676
8.	670	23.	520
9.	26	24.	602
10.	189	25.	152
11.	701	26.	154
12.	71	27.	38
13.	170	28.	153
14.	62	29.	863
15.	599	30.	599

Mental Math 16			
1.	27	16.	100
2.	200	17.	583
3.	58	18.	127
4.	95	19.	292
5.	1000	20.	930
6.	23	21.	65
7.	430	22.	53
8.	689	23.	305
9.	382	24.	784
10.	297	25.	863
11.	369	26.	489
12.	516	27.	211
13.	533	28.	695
14.	560	29.	72
15.	922	30.	752

Mental Math 17		
1.	881	
2.	312	
3.	340	
4.	566	
5.	127	
6.	114	
7.	300	
8.	163	
9.	765	
10.	67	
11.	600	
12.	24	
13.	30	
14.	16	
15.	65	

Mental Math 20			
1.	8	16.	24
2.	36	17.	40
3.	24	18.	8
4.	28	19.	32
5.	24	20.	12
6.	12	21.	40
7.	28	22.	36
8.	40	23.	16
9.	20	24.	32
10.	32	25.	20
11.	20	26.	20
12.	36	27.	28
13.	16	28.	40
14.	28	29.	36
15.	32	30.	24

Mental Math 18

x	1	2	3	4	5	6	7	8	9	10
1	1	2	3	4	5	6	7	8	9	10
2	2	4	6	8	10	12	14	16	18	20
3	3	6	9	12	15	18	21	24	27	30
4	4	8	12	16	20	24	28	32	36	40
5	5	10	15	20						
6	6	12	18	24						
7	7	14	21	28						
8	8	16	24	32						
9	9	18	27	36						
10	10	20	30	40						

Mental Math 19

x	5	10	2	1	8	9	3	7	4	6
2	10	20	4	2	16	18	6	14	8	12
3	15	30	6	3	24	27	9	21	12	18
4	20	40	8	4	32	36	12	28	16	24

x	3	6	1	9	5	4	7	10	8	2
4	12	24	4	36	20	16	28	40	32	8
2	6	12	2	18	10	8	14	20	16	4
3	9	18	3	27	15	12	21	30	24	6

x	1	4	5	2	7	3	8	9	6	10
3	3	12	15	6	21	9	24	27	18	30
4	4	16	20	8	28	12	32	36	24	40
2	2	8	10	4	14	6	16	18	12	20

Mental Math 21			
1.	3	16.	7
2.	1	17.	4
3.	9	18.	2
4.	6	19.	4
5.	5	20.	5
6.	8	21.	6
7.	6	22.	9
8.	10	23.	7
9.	5	24.	7
10.	3	25.	2
11.	8	26.	9
12.	1	27.	8
13.	4	28.	10
14.	9	29.	3
15.	6	30.	10

Mental Math 24			
1.	5	16.	50
2.	35	17.	35
3.	20	18.	5
4.	35	19.	40
5.	10	20.	20
6.	50	21.	30
7.	40	22.	35
8.	25	23.	30
9.	40	24.	45
10.	50	25.	40
11.	15	26.	25
12.	30	27.	45
13.	45	28.	25
14.	45	29.	40
15.	20	30.	50

Mental Math 22

x	1	2	3	4	5	6	7	8	9	10
1	1	2	3	4	5	6	7	8	9	10
2	2	4	6	8	10	12	14	16	18	20
3	3	6	9	12	15	18	21	24	27	30
4	4	8	12	16	20	24	28	32	36	40
5	5	10	15	20	25	30	35	40	45	50
6	6	12	18	24	30					
7	7	14	21	28	35					
8	8	16	24	32	40					
9	9	18	27	36	45					
10	10	20	30	40	50					

Mental Math 23

x	5	10	2	1	8	9	3	7	4	6
3	15	30	6	3	24	27	9	21	12	18
4	20	40	8	4	32	36	12	28	16	24
5	25	50	10	5	40	45	15	35	20	30

x	3	6	1	9	5	4	7	10	8	2
5	15	30	5	45	25	20	35	50	40	10
3	9	18	3	27	15	12	21	30	24	6
4	12	24	4	36	20	16	28	40	32	8

x	1	4	5	2	7	3	8	9	6	10
4	4	16	20	8	28	12	32	36	24	40
5	5	20	25	10	35	15	40	45	30	50
3	3	12	15	6	21	9	24	27	18	30

Mental Math 25

#		#	
1.	1	16.	10
2.	5	17.	9
3.	9	18.	2
4.	9	19.	8
5.	8	20.	3
6.	4	21.	6
7.	2	22.	5
8.	7	23.	6
9.	3	24.	5
10.	5	25.	4
11.	5	26.	7
12.	6	27.	9
13.	4	28.	6
14.	7	29.	7
15.	9	30.	10

Mental Math 27

#		#	
1.	3	16.	36
2.	7	17.	28
3.	45	18.	32
4.	20	19.	4
5.	5	20.	50
6.	8	21.	6
7.	32	22.	40
8.	16	23.	6
9.	5	24.	25
10.	30	25.	8
11.	8	26.	4
12.	9	27.	9
13.	24	28.	7
14.	40	29.	2
15.	15	30.	35

Mental Math 28

#		#	
1.	45	16.	6
2.	25	17.	3
3.	7	18.	8
4.	9	19.	4
5.	4	20.	10
6.	90	21.	10
7.	3	22.	8
8.	20	23.	9
9.	6	24.	7
10.	35	25.	6
11.	12	26.	9
12.	4	27.	18
13.	28	28.	5
14.	100	29.	80
15.	60	30.	8

Mental Math 26

x	1	2	3	4	5	6	7	8	9	10
1	1	2	3	4	5	6	7	8	9	10
2	2	4	6	8	10	12	14	16	18	20
3	3	6	9	12	15	18	21	24	27	30
4	4	8	12	16	20	24	28	32	36	40
5	5	10	15	20	25	30	35	40	45	50
6	6	12	18	24	30					60
7	7	14	21	28	35					70
8	8	16	24	32	40					80
9	9	18	27	36	45					90
10	10	20	30	40	50	60	70	80	90	100

Mental Math 29

#		#	
1.	25	16.	2
2.	50	17.	4
3.	65	18.	8.60
4.	15	19.	2
5.	30	20.	2.72
6.	93	21.	10
7.	6.15	22.	8
8.	5.60	23.	5.50
9.	7.70	24.	7.39
10.	7.40	25.	3.24
11.	1.65	26.	6.38
12.	7.40	27.	8.21
13.	5.65	28.	9.15
14.	6.65	29.	9.34
15.	7.32	30.	9

Mental Math 30

#		#	
1.	4.60	16.	4.61
2.	2.15	17.	3.37
3.	2.35	18.	1.88
4.	3.25	19.	6.27
5.	7.77	20.	2.68
6.	4.58	21.	1.90
7.	3.10	22.	3.79
8.	2.80	23.	10
9.	2.20	24.	2.10
10.	5.67	25.	8.64
11.	3.71	26.	3.74
12.	34	27.	8.31
13.	88	28.	4.37
14.	289	29.	446
15.	558	30.	231

Mental Math 1

1. $100 - 25 = $ _____

2. $100 - 50 = $ _____

3. $100 - 75 = $ _____

4. $100 - 99 = $ _____

5. $100 - 5 = $ _____

6. $100 - 60 = $ _____

7. $100 - 38 = $ _____

8. $100 - 45 = $ _____

9. $100 - 44 = $ _____

10. $100 - 10 = $ _____

11. $100 - 87 = $ _____

12. $100 - 22 = $ _____

13. $100 - 4 = $ _____

14. $100 - 69 = $ _____

15. $37 + $ _____ $= 100$

16. $76 + $ _____ $= 100$

17. $51 + $ _____ $= 100$

18. $40 + $ _____ $= 100$

19. _____ $+ 90 = 100$

20. _____ $+ 55 = 100$

21. _____ $+ 7 = 100$

22. _____ $+ 33 = 100$

23. $100 - $ _____ $= 80$

24. $100 - $ _____ $= 41$

25. $100 - $ _____ $= 82$

26. $100 - $ _____ $= 57$

27. $100 - $ _____ $= 18$

28. $100 - $ _____ $= 71$

Finish the pattern:

4, 8, _____ , 16, _____ , 24, _____ , 32, _____ , 40

Mental Math 2

1. $100 - 95 = $ _____

2. $100 - 70 = $ _____

3. $85 + $ _____ $ = 100$

4. _____ $ + 13 = 100$

5. _____ $ + 35 = 100$

6. $100 - 20 = $ _____

7. $18 + $ _____ $ = 100$

8. $100 - 77 = $ _____

9. $100 - $ _____ $ = 3$

10. $100 - 29 = $ _____

11. $100 - 66 = $ _____

12. $100 - $ _____ $ = 98$

13. _____ $ + 88 = 100$

14. $84 + $ _____ $ = 100$

15. $100 - 65 = $ _____

16. $25 + $ _____ $ = 100$

17. $100 - 30 = $ _____

18. $8 + $ _____ $ = 100$

19. _____ $ + 50 = 100$

20. $100 - 15 = $ _____

21. $100 - 72 = $ _____

22. _____ $ + 46 = 100$

23. $100 - $ _____ $ = 75$

24. $100 - 31 = $ _____

25. $75 + 25 + 94 = $ _____

26. $69 + 27 + 31 = $ _____

27. $54 + 46 + $ _____ $ = 119$

28. $57 + 72 + $ _____ $ = 157$

Finish the pattern:

4, 8, _____ , _____ , _____ , _____ , _____ , _____ , _____ , _____

Mental Math 3

1. $24 + 7 =$ _____
2. $72 + 5 =$ _____
3. $65 + 6 =$ _____
4. $59 + 5 =$ _____
5. $66 + 7 =$ _____
6. $25 + 6 =$ _____
7. $64 + 9 =$ _____
8. $77 + 8 =$ _____
9. $71 + 9 =$ _____
10. $35 + 8 =$ _____
11. $57 + 5 =$ _____
12. $35 + 5 =$ _____
13. $56 + 9 =$ _____
14. $42 + 6 =$ _____

15. $86 + 6 =$ _____
16. $59 + 7 =$ _____
17. $37 + 3 =$ _____
18. $79 + 3 =$ _____
19. $28 + 6 =$ _____
20. $37 + 7 =$ _____
21. $18 + 9 =$ _____
22. $73 + 8 =$ _____
23. $28 + 2 =$ _____
24. $69 + 9 =$ _____
25. $36 + 4 =$ _____
26. $58 + 4 =$ _____
27. $82 + 9 =$ _____
28. $91 + 9 =$ _____

Finish the pattern:

5, 10, _____ , 20, _____ , _____, 35 , _____, _____ , _____

Mental Math 4

1. $18 + 80 =$ _____
2. $42 + 20 =$ _____
3. $68 + 20 =$ _____
4. $72 + 10 =$ _____
5. $88 + 20 =$ _____
6. $12 + 80 =$ _____
7. $54 + 90 =$ _____
8. $86 + 20 =$ _____
9. $32 + 50 =$ _____
10. $52 + 60 =$ _____
11. $77 + 70 =$ _____
12. $82 + 40 =$ _____
13. $60 + 60 =$ _____
14. $78 + 90 =$ _____

15. $87 + 50 =$ _____
16. $60 + 70 =$ _____
17. $70 + 80 =$ _____
18. $85 + 30 =$ _____
19. $56 + 90 =$ _____
20. $74 + 40 =$ _____
21. $68 + 90 =$ _____
22. $63 + 50 =$ _____
23. $80 + 60 =$ _____
24. $60 + 70 =$ _____
25. $72 + 50 =$ _____
26. $50 + 80 =$ _____
27. $68 + 80 =$ _____
28. $74 + 60 =$ _____

Finish the pattern:

5, 10, ___ , ___ , ___ , ___ , ___ , ___ , ___ , ___

Mental Math 5

1. 432 + 4 = _____   15. 618 + 5 = _____

2. 216 + 4 = _____   16. 526 + 7 = _____

3. 724 + 4 = _____   17. 857 + 8 = _____

4. 908 + 4 = _____   18. 148 + 2 = _____

5. 112 + 4 = _____   19. 493 + 4 = _____

6. 309 + 1 = _____   20. 307 + 4 = _____

7. 504 + 9 = _____   21. 216 + 9 = _____

8. 758 + 2 = _____   22. 626 + 3 = _____

9. 848 + 2 = _____   23. 538 + 6 = _____

10. 285 + 6 = _____   24. 876 + 7 = _____

11. 847 + 7 = _____   25. 207 + 3 = _____

12. 258 + 4 = _____   26. 315 + 8 = _____

13. 185 + 7 = _____   27. 123 + 7 = _____

14. 987 + 8 = _____   28. 389 + 4 = _____

Finish the pattern:

40, _____ , 32, _____ , _____ , 20, _____ , _____ , 8, 4

Mental Math 6

1. $614 + 80 =$ _____

2. $248 + 20 =$ _____

3. $160 + 60 =$ _____

4. $972 + 10 =$ _____

5. $622 + 70 =$ _____

6. $126 + 20 =$ _____

7. $541 + 40 =$ _____

8. $269 + 20 =$ _____

9. $370 + 50 =$ _____

10. $452 + 60 =$ _____

11. $778 + 70 =$ _____

12. $285 + 40 =$ _____

13. $364 + 60 =$ _____

14. $570 + 90 =$ _____

15. $285 + 50 =$ _____

16. $861 + 70 =$ _____

17. $477 + 80 =$ _____

18. $186 + 30 =$ _____

19. $259 + 90 =$ _____

20. $770 + 40 =$ _____

21. $662 + 90 =$ _____

22. $361 + 50 =$ _____

23. $880 + 60 =$ _____

24. $262 + 70 =$ _____

25. $671 + 50 =$ _____

26. $253 + 80 =$ _____

27. $167 + 80 =$ _____

28. $473 + 60 =$ _____

Finish the pattern:

50, 45 , ___ , ___ , ___ , ___ , ___ , ___ , ___ , ___

Mental Math 7

1. $24 + 72 =$ _____
2. $72 + 15 =$ _____
3. $65 + 32 =$ _____
4. $53 + 45 =$ _____
5. $66 + 32 =$ _____
6. $25 + 62 =$ _____
7. $64 + 12 =$ _____
8. $71 + 28 =$ _____
9. $17 + 82 =$ _____
10. $35 + 63 =$ _____
11. $57 + 41 =$ _____
12. $35 + 5 =$ _____
13. $16 + 73 =$ _____
14. $41 + 26 =$ _____
15. $82 + 11 =$ _____
16. $281 + 16 =$ _____
17. $452 + 24 =$ _____
18. $137 + 31 =$ _____
19. $172 + 28 =$ _____
20. $927 + 62 =$ _____
21. $637 + 41 =$ _____
22. $108 + 800 =$ _____
23. $232 + 600 =$ _____
24. $448 + 500 =$ _____
25. $105 + 500 =$ _____
26. $136 + 400 =$ _____
27. $758 + 200 =$ _____
28. $412 + 300 =$ _____
29. $111 + 700 =$ _____
30. $626 + 300 =$ _____

Mental Math 8

1. $24 + 99 =$ _____
2. $25 + 98 =$ _____
3. $5 + 98 =$ _____
4. $32 + 99 =$ _____
5. $67 + 99 =$ _____
6. $25 + 98 =$ _____
7. $42 + 98 =$ _____
8. $71 + 98 =$ _____
9. $62 + 99 =$ _____
10. $45 + 98 =$ _____
11. $97 + 99 =$ _____
12. $325 + 99 =$ _____
13. $216 + 99 =$ _____
14. $641 + 98 =$ _____
15. $812 + 99 =$ _____

16. $99 + 416 =$ _____
17. $98 + 234 =$ _____
18. $367 + 99 =$ _____
19. $98 + 238 =$ _____
21. $99 + 602 =$ _____
22. $99 + 481 =$ _____
23. $182 + 98 =$ _____
24. $324 + 99 =$ _____
23. $98 + 691 =$ _____
25. $99 + 304 =$ _____
26. $126 + 98 =$ _____
27. $99 + 412 =$ _____
28. $198 + 626 =$ _____
29. $95 + 198 =$ _____
30. $428 + 299 =$ _____

Mental Math 9

1. $60 + 77 =$ _____

2. $32 + 28 =$ _____

3. $68 + 7 =$ _____

4. $22 + 99 =$ _____

5. $500 + 350 =$ _____

6. $135 + 8 =$ _____

7. $638 + 90 =$ _____

8. $55 + 45 =$ _____

9. $99 + 258 =$ _____

10. $182 + 16 =$ _____

11. $45 + 23 =$ _____

12. $650 + 20 =$ _____

13. $98 + 281 =$ _____

14. $308 + 99 =$ _____

15. $281 + 704 =$ _____

16. $5 + 208 =$ _____

17. $70 + 165 =$ _____

18. $463 + 99 =$ _____

19. $62 + 50 =$ _____

20. $32 + 68 =$ _____

21. $158 + 98 =$ _____

22. $480 + 50 =$ _____

23. $365 + 80 =$ _____

24. $601 + 200 =$ _____

25. $98 + 198 =$ _____

26. $64 + 36 =$ _____

27. $98 + 6 =$ _____

28. $41 + 258 =$ _____

29. $99 + 62 =$ _____

30. $650 + 242 =$ _____

Mental Math 10

1. $91 - 9 =$ _____

2. $34 - 8 =$ _____

3. $22 - 7 =$ _____

4. $75 - 9 =$ _____

5. $83 - 5 =$ _____

6. $26 - 7 =$ _____

7. $63 - 7 =$ _____

8. $64 - 6 =$ _____

9. $52 - 8 =$ _____

10. $93 - 6 =$ _____

11. $44 - 5 =$ _____

12. $31 - 8 =$ _____

13. $51 - 5 =$ _____

14. $76 - 9 =$ _____

15. $82 - 3 =$ _____

16. $41 - 6 =$ _____

17. $84 - 9 =$ _____

18. $31 - 7 =$ _____

19. $97 - 9 =$ _____

20. $66 - 8 =$ _____

21. $73 - 8 =$ _____

22. $52 - 5 =$ _____

23. $54 - 7 =$ _____

24. $23 - 9 =$ _____

25. $85 - 8 =$ _____

26. $42 - 6 =$ _____

27. $35 - 6 =$ _____

28. $72 - 9 =$ _____

29. $47 - 8 =$ _____

30. $41 - 2 =$ _____

Mental Math 11

1. 291 − 9 = _____
2. 534 − 8 = _____
3. 122 − 7 = _____
4. 975 − 9 = _____
5. 823 − 5 = _____
6. 426 − 7 = _____
7. 653 − 7 = _____
8. 364 − 6 = _____
9. 752 − 8 = _____
10. 373 − 6 = _____
11. 244 − 5 = _____
12. 481 − 8 = _____
13. 551 − 5 = _____
14. 176 − 9 = _____
15. 665 − 7 = _____
16. 41 − 6 = _____
17. 884 − 9 = _____
18. 391 − 7 = _____
19. 927 − 9 = _____
20. 646 − 8 = _____
21. 713 − 8 = _____
22. 552 − 5 = _____
23. 954 − 7 = _____
24. 823 − 9 = _____
25. 865 − 8 = _____
26. 422 − 6 = _____
27. 430 − 6 = _____
28. 272 − 9 = _____
29. 420 − 8 = _____
30. 208 − 8 = _____

Mental Math 12

1. $288 - 20 =$ _____
2. $841 - 20 =$ _____
3. $621 - 20 =$ _____
4. $398 - 40 =$ _____
5. $792 - 30 =$ _____
6. $610 - 50 =$ _____
7. $770 - 40 =$ _____
8. $240 - 80 =$ _____
9. $730 - 70 =$ _____
10. $400 - 70 =$ _____
11. $610 - 60 =$ _____
12. $920 - 50 =$ _____
13. $510 - 90 =$ _____
14. $420 - 80 =$ _____
15. $210 - 20 =$ _____
16. $520 - 60 =$ _____
17. $220 - 70 =$ _____
18. $410 - 80 =$ _____
19. $700 - 60 =$ _____
20. $530 - 70 =$ _____
21. $620 - 40 =$ _____
22. $112 - 50 =$ _____
23. $537 - 60 =$ _____
24. $720 - 300 =$ _____
25. $930 - 200 =$ _____
26. $123 - 90 =$ _____
27. $632 - 400 =$ _____
28. $716 - 200 =$ _____
29. $132 - 90 =$ _____
30. $220 - 30 =$ _____

Mental Math 13

1. $99 - 20 =$ _____

2. $34 - 10 =$ _____

3. $82 - 40 =$ _____

4. $75 - 30 =$ _____

5. $83 - 50 =$ _____

6. $86 - 70 =$ _____

7. $65 - 52 =$ _____

8. $64 - 61 =$ _____

9. $57 - 35 =$ _____

10. $93 - 62 =$ _____

11. $84 - 51 =$ _____

12. $96 - 74 =$ _____

13. $88 - 51 =$ _____

14. $96 - 35 =$ _____

15. $82 - 41 =$ _____

16. $47 - 26 =$ _____

17. $89 - 54 =$ _____

18. $96 - 72 =$ _____

19. $27 - 14 =$ _____

20. $86 - 22 =$ _____

21. $78 - 36 =$ _____

22. $58 - 51 =$ _____

23. $74 - 52 =$ _____

24. $93 - 61 =$ _____

25. $85 - 55 =$ _____

26. $48 - 16 =$ _____

27. $35 - 11 =$ _____

28. $72 - 52 =$ _____

29. $47 - 16 =$ _____

30. $94 - 32 =$ _____

Mental Math 14

1. $200 - 99 =$ _____
2. $400 - 98 =$ _____
3. $600 - 99 =$ _____
4. $500 - 99 =$ _____
5. $100 - 98 =$ _____
6. $800 - 99 =$ _____
7. $360 - 98 =$ _____
8. $730 - 98 =$ _____
9. $910 - 98 =$ _____
10. $620 - 99 =$ _____
11. $431 - 98 =$ _____
12. $698 - 98 =$ _____
13. $843 - 99 =$ _____
14. $251 - 98 =$ _____
15. $432 - 98 =$ _____

16. $365 - 99 =$ _____
17. $785 - 98 =$ _____
18. $256 - 99 =$ _____
19. $258 - 98 =$ _____
20. $762 - 98 =$ _____
21. $365 - 99 =$ _____
22. $258 - 99 =$ _____
23. $204 - 99 =$ _____
24. $560 - 99 =$ _____
25. $701 - 98 =$ _____
26. $584 - 98 =$ _____
27. $887 - 199 =$ _____
28. $963 - 298 =$ _____
29. $514 - 399 =$ _____
30. $681 - 599 =$ _____

Mental Math 15

1. $100 - 75 =$ _____

2. $82 - 5 =$ _____

3. $584 - 99 =$ _____

4. $96 - 33 =$ _____

5. $582 - 9 =$ _____

6. $250 - 60 =$ _____

7. $986 - 400 =$ _____

8. $690 - 20 =$ _____

9. $86 - 60 =$ _____

10. $287 - 98 =$ _____

11. $800 - 99 =$ _____

12. $87 - 16 =$ _____

13. $240 - 70 =$ _____

14. $100 - 38 =$ _____

15. $698 - 99 =$ _____

16. $78 - 30 =$ _____

17. $380 - 200 =$ _____

18. $62 - 8 =$ _____

19. $24 - 6 =$ _____

20. $687 - 99 =$ _____

21. $412 - 8 =$ _____

22. $683 - 7 =$ _____

23. $610 - 90 =$ _____

24. $700 - 98 =$ _____

25. $250 - 98 =$ _____

26. $254 - 100 =$ _____

27. $100 - 62 =$ _____

28. $754 - 601 =$ _____

29. $986 - 123 =$ _____

30. $697 - 98 =$ _____

Mental Math 16

1. $32 - 5 =$ _____

2. $120 + 80 =$ _____

3. $88 - 30 =$ _____

4. $34 + 61 =$ _____

5. $960 + 40 =$ _____

6. $100 - 77 =$ _____

7. $340 + 90 =$ _____

8. $289 + 400 =$ _____

9. $284 + 98 =$ _____

10. $306 - 9 =$ _____

11. $362 + 7 =$ _____

12. $417 + 99 =$ _____

13. $632 - 99 =$ _____

14. $640 - 80 =$ _____

15. $982 - 60 =$ _____

16. $42 + 58 =$ _____

17. $633 - 50 =$ _____

18. $67 + 60 =$ _____

19. $391 - 99 =$ _____

20. $300 + 630 =$ _____

21. $58 + 7 =$ _____

22. $85 - 32 =$ _____

23. $235 + 70 =$ _____

24. $984 - 200 =$ _____

25. $984 - 121 =$ _____

26. $587 - 98 =$ _____

27. $203 + 8 =$ _____

28. $698 - 3 =$ _____

29. $100 - 28 =$ _____

30. $98 + 654 =$ _____

Mental Math 17

1. $834 + 7 - 20 + 60 =$ _____

2. $368 - 99 + 40 + 3 =$ _____

3. $429 + 8 - 7 - 90 =$ _____

4. $501 - 4 - 30 + 99 =$ _____

5. $87 + 7 + 2 - 9 + 40 =$ _____

6. $4 + 4 + 4 + 4 + 98 =$ _____

7. $5 + 5 + 5 + 5 + 280 =$ _____

8. $33 + 21 + 9 - 30 + 130 =$ _____

9. $925 - 98 + 3 - 70 + 5 =$ _____

10. $62 + 8 - 2 + 40 - 8 - 33 =$ _____

11. $592 + 99 - 98 + 7 =$ _____

12. $4 + 4 + 4 + 4 + 4 + 4 =$ _____

13. $5 + 5 + 5 + 5 + 5 + 5 =$ _____

14. $40 - 4 - 4 - 4 - 4 - 4 - 4 =$ _____

15. $2 + 3 + 4 + 5 + 6 + 7 + 8 + 9 + 10 + 11 =$ _____

Mental Math 18

X	1	2	3	4	5	6	7	8	9	10
1										
2										
3										
4										
5										
6										
7										
8										
9										
10										

Mental Math 19

X	5	10	2	1	8	9	3	7	4	6
2										
3										
4										

X	3	6	1	9	5	4	7	10	8	2
4										
2										
3										

X	1	4	5	2	7	3	8	9	6	10
3										
4										
2										

Mental Math 20

1. $2 \times 4 =$ _____

2. $4 \times 9 =$ _____

3. $6 \times 4 =$ _____

4. $4 \times 7 =$ _____

5. $6 \times 4 =$ _____

6. $4 \times 3 =$ _____

7. $7 \times 4 =$ _____

8. $4 \times 10 =$ _____

9. $4 \times 5 =$ _____

10. $8 \times 4 =$ _____

11. $5 \times 4 =$ _____

12. $4 \times 9 =$ _____

13. $4 \times 4 =$ _____

14. $7 \times 4 =$ _____

15. $4 \times 8 =$ _____

16. $4 \times 6 =$ _____

17. $4 \times 10 =$ _____

18. $4 \times 2 =$ _____

19. $8 \times 4 =$ _____

20. $3 \times 4 =$ _____

21. $10 \times 4 =$ _____

22. $9 \times 4 =$ _____

23. $4 \times 4 =$ _____

24. $4 \times 8 =$ _____

25. $4 \times 5 =$ _____

26. $5 \times 4 =$ _____

27. $4 \times 7 =$ _____

28. $10 \times 4 =$ _____

29. $9 \times 4 =$ _____

30. $4 \times 6 =$ _____

Mental Math 21

1. $12 \div 4 =$ _____

2. $4 \div 4 =$ _____

3. $36 \div 4 =$ _____

4. $24 \div 4 =$ _____

5. $15 \div 3 =$ _____

6. $32 \div 4 =$ _____

7. $18 \div 3 =$ _____

8. $40 \div 4 =$ _____

9. $20 \div 4 =$ _____

10. $9 \div 3 =$ _____

11. $24 \div 3 =$ _____

12. $4 \div 4 =$ _____

13. $16 \div 4 =$ _____

14. $27 \div 3 =$ _____

15. $24 \div 4 =$ _____

16. $28 \div 4 =$ _____

17. $16 \div 4 =$ _____

18. $8 \div 4 =$ _____

19. $12 \div 3 =$ _____

20. $20 \div 4 =$ _____

21. $24 \div 4 =$ _____

22. $36 \div 4 =$ _____

23. $28 \div 4 =$ _____

24. $21 \div 3 =$ _____

25. $8 \div 4 =$ _____

26. $36 \div 4 =$ _____

27. $32 \div 4 =$ _____

28. $30 \div 3 =$ _____

29. $12 \div 4 =$ _____

30. $40 \div 4 =$ _____

Mental Math 22

X	1	2	3	4	5	6	7	8	9	10
1										
2										
3										
4										
5										
6										
7										
8										
9										
10										

Mental Math 23

X	5	10	2	1	8	9	3	7	4	6
3										
4										
5										

X	3	6	1	9	5	4	7	10	8	2
5										
3										
4										

X	1	4	5	2	7	3	8	9	6	10
4										
5										
3										

Mental Math 24

1. $1 \times 5 = \underline{\hspace{1cm}}$

2. $5 \times 7 = \underline{\hspace{1cm}}$

3. $4 \times 5 = \underline{\hspace{1cm}}$

4. $5 \times 7 = \underline{\hspace{1cm}}$

5. $2 \times 5 = \underline{\hspace{1cm}}$

6. $5 \times 10 = \underline{\hspace{1cm}}$

7. $8 \times 5 = \underline{\hspace{1cm}}$

8. $5 \times 5 = \underline{\hspace{1cm}}$

9. $5 \times 8 = \underline{\hspace{1cm}}$

10. $5 \times 10 = \underline{\hspace{1cm}}$

11. $3 \times 5 = \underline{\hspace{1cm}}$

12. $5 \times 6 = \underline{\hspace{1cm}}$

13. $5 \times 9 = \underline{\hspace{1cm}}$

14. $9 \times 5 = \underline{\hspace{1cm}}$

15. $5 \times 4 = \underline{\hspace{1cm}}$

16. $10 \times 5 = \underline{\hspace{1cm}}$

17. $7 \times 5 = \underline{\hspace{1cm}}$

18. $5 \times 1 = \underline{\hspace{1cm}}$

19. $5 \times 8 = \underline{\hspace{1cm}}$

20. $5 \times 4 = \underline{\hspace{1cm}}$

21. $5 \times 6 = \underline{\hspace{1cm}}$

22. $7 \times 5 = \underline{\hspace{1cm}}$

23. $6 \times 5 = \underline{\hspace{1cm}}$

24. $5 \times 9 = \underline{\hspace{1cm}}$

25. $8 \times 5 = \underline{\hspace{1cm}}$

26. $5 \times 5 = \underline{\hspace{1cm}}$

27. $9 \times 5 = \underline{\hspace{1cm}}$

28. $5 \times 5 = \underline{\hspace{1cm}}$

29. $5 \times 8 = \underline{\hspace{1cm}}$

30. $10 \times 5 = \underline{\hspace{1cm}}$

Mental Math 25

1. $5 \div 5 =$ _____

2. $25 \div 5 =$ _____

3. $36 \div 4 =$ _____

4. $45 \div 5 =$ _____

5. $32 \div 4 =$ _____

6. $20 \div 5 =$ _____

7. $10 \div 5 =$ _____

8. $35 \div 5 =$ _____

9. $15 \div 5 =$ _____

10. $25 \div 5 =$ _____

11. $15 \div 3 =$ _____

12. $30 \div 5 =$ _____

13. $16 \div 4 =$ _____

14. $21 \div 3 =$ _____

15. $45 \div 5 =$ _____

16. $50 \div 5 =$ _____

17. $27 \div 3 =$ _____

18. $10 \div 5 =$ _____

19. $40 \div 5 =$ _____

20. $15 \div 5 =$ _____

21. $24 \div 4 =$ _____

22. $25 \div 5 =$ _____

23. $30 \div 5 =$ _____

24. $20 \div 4 =$ _____

25. $20 \div 5 =$ _____

26. $35 \div 5 =$ _____

27. $45 \div 5 =$ _____

28. $24 \div 4 =$ _____

29. $28 \div 4 =$ _____

30. $50 \div 5 =$ _____

Mental Math 26

X	1	2	3	4	5	6	7	8	9	10
1										
2										
3										
4										
5										
6										
7										
8										
9										
10										

Mental Math 27

1. $15 \div 5 =$ _____

2. $28 \div 4 =$ _____

3. $5 \times 9 =$ _____

4. $4 \times 5 =$ _____

5. $20 \div 4 =$ _____

6. $32 \div 4 =$ _____

7. $8 \times 4 =$ _____

8. $4 \times 4 =$ _____

9. $25 \div 5 =$ _____

10. $6 \times 5 =$ _____

11. $4 \times 2 =$ _____

12. $45 \div 5 =$ _____

13. $4 \times 6 =$ _____

14. $10 \times 4 =$ _____

15. $3 \times 5 =$ _____

16. $9 \times 4 =$ _____

17. $7 \times 4 =$ _____

18. $4 \times 8 =$ _____

19. $20 \div 5 =$ _____

20. $10 \times 5 =$ _____

21. $24 \div 4 =$ _____

22. $8 \times 5 =$ _____

23. $30 \div 5 =$ _____

24. $5 \times 5 =$ _____

25. $40 \div 5 =$ _____

26. $16 \div 4 =$ _____

27. $36 \div 4 =$ _____

28. $35 \div 5 =$ _____

29. $10 \div 5 =$ _____

30. $5 \times 7 =$ _____

Mental Math 28

1. $5 \times 9 =$ _____

2. $5 \times 5 =$ _____

3. $70 \div 10 =$ _____

4. $27 \div 3 =$ _____

5. $2 \times 2 =$ _____

6. $10 \times 9 =$ _____

7. $9 \div 3 =$ _____

8. $5 \times 4 =$ _____

9. $18 \div 3 =$ _____

10. $5 \times 7 =$ _____

11. $4 \times 3 =$ _____

12. $12 \div 3 =$ _____

13. $4 \times 7 =$ _____

14. $10 \times 10 =$ _____

15. $6 \times 10 =$ _____

16. $2 \times 3 =$ _____

17. $12 \div 4 =$ _____

18. $80 \div 10 =$ _____

19. $8 \div 2 =$ _____

20. $2 \times 5 =$ _____

21. $100 \div 10 =$ _____

22. $24 \div 3 =$ _____

23. $27 \div 3 =$ _____

24. $21 \div 3 =$ _____

25. $24 \div 4 =$ _____

26. $3 \times 3 =$ _____

27. $3 \times 6 =$ _____

28. $15 \div 3 =$ _____

29. $8 \times 10 =$ _____

30. $32 \div 4 =$ _____

Mental Math 29

1. $1 – 75¢ = _____ ¢

2. $1 – 50¢ = _____ ¢

3. $1 – 35¢ = _____ ¢

4. 85¢ + _____ ¢ = $1

5. 70¢ + _____ ¢ = $1

6. 7¢ + _____ ¢ = $1

7. $10 - $3.85 = $_____

8. $10 - $4.40 = $_____

9. $10 - $2.30 = $_____

10. $2.60 + $_____ = $10

11. $8.35 + $_____ = $10

12. $2.60 + $_____ = $10

13. $2.65 + $3 = $_____

14. $2.65 + $4 = $_____

15. $5.32 + $2 = $_____

16. $1.25 + 75¢ = $_____

17. $3.45 + 55¢ = $_____

18. $8.35 + 25¢ = $_____

19. $1.75 + 25¢ = $_____

20. $2.40 + 32¢ = $_____

21. $9.20 + 80¢ = $_____

22. $3.60 + $4.40 = $_____

23. $3.35 + $2.15 = $_____

24. $6.40 + $0.99 = $_____

25. $2.25 + $0.99 = $_____

26. $2.40 + $3.98 = $_____

27. $6.24 + $1.97 = $_____

28. $2.20 + $6.95 = $_____

29. $4.35 + $4.99 = $_____

30. $2.05 + $6.95 = $_____

Mental Math 30

1. $8.60 – $4 = $_____

2. $5.15 – $3 = $_____

3. $9.35 – $7 = $_____

4. $4 – 75¢ = $_____

5. $8 – 23¢ = $_____

6. $5 – 42¢ = $_____

7. $4.90 – $1.80 = $____

8. $8.85 – $6.05 = $____

9. $3.45 – $1.25 = $____

10. $9.99 – $4.32 = $____

11. $7.00 – $3.29 = $____

12. $42 – $8 = $_____

13. $95 – $7 = $_____

14. $387 – $98 = $_____

15. $600 – $42 = $_____

16. $5.60 – $0.99 = $____

17. $4.35 – $0.98 = $____

18. $2.85 – $0.97 = $____

19. $7.23 – $0.96 = $____

20. $3.63 – $0.95 = $____

21. $5.85 – $3.95 = $____

22. $6.74 – $2.95 = $____

23. $3.05 + $6.95 = $____

24. $9.05 – $6.95 = $____

25. $4.69 + $3.95 = $____

26. $7.69 – $3.95 = $____

27. $6.34 + $1.97 = $____

28. $6.34 – $1.97 = $____

29. $348 + $98 = $_____

30. $329 – $98 = $_____

U.S. Measurement Review

1. Fill in the blanks with yd (yard), ft (feet) or in (inches)

    (a) The width of a door is about 1 _____.

    (b) Paul is 4 _____ shorter than his brother.

    (c) The room is about 20 _____ long.

    (d) George took part in a 100 _____ dash.

2. Fill in the blanks with lb (pound) or oz (ounce)

    (a) A watermelon weighs about 4 _____.

    (b) A pear weighs about 5 _____.

    (c) Joan bought a bottle of honey that weighed 1 _____.

    (d) Mrs. Mbele bought a 5 _____ bag of rice.

3. Mary weighs 62 pounds. Her sister weighs 14 pounds less. How much does her sister weigh?

4. Two blocks and a toy car weigh 15 ounces. The toy car weighs 3 ounces.
    (a) How much do the two blocks weigh?

    (b) How much does one block weigh?

5. Draw a line that is 8 inches long.

Appendix

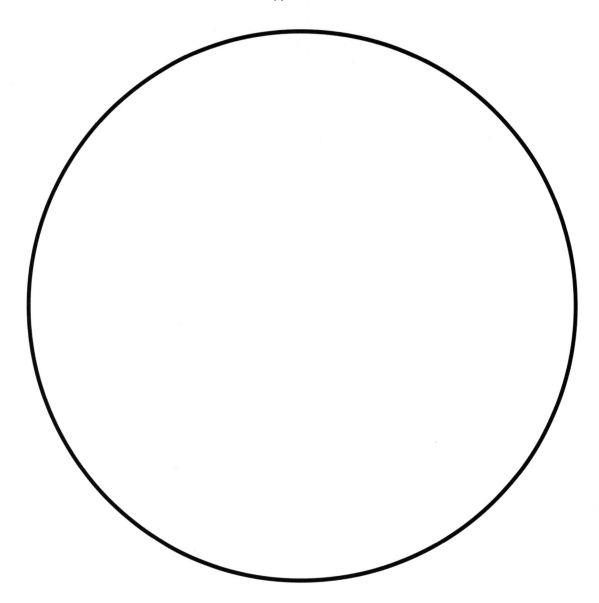

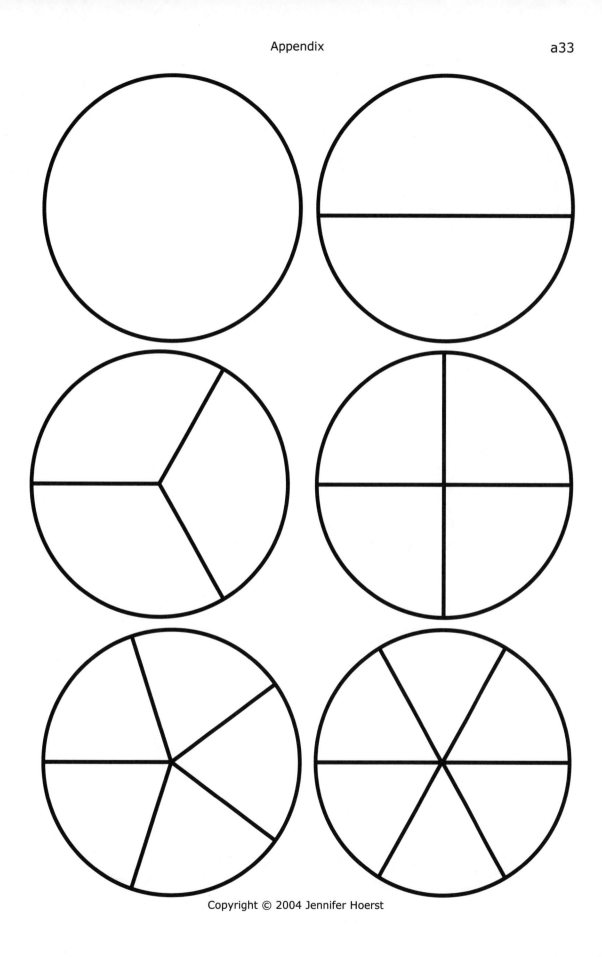

1											

| $\frac{1}{2}$ | | | | | | $\frac{1}{2}$ | | | | | |

| $\frac{1}{3}$ | | | | $\frac{1}{3}$ | | | | $\frac{1}{3}$ | | | |

| $\frac{1}{4}$ | | | $\frac{1}{4}$ | | | $\frac{1}{4}$ | | | $\frac{1}{4}$ | | |

| $\frac{1}{5}$ | | $\frac{1}{5}$ | | $\frac{1}{5}$ | | $\frac{1}{5}$ | | $\frac{1}{5}$ | | | |

| $\frac{1}{6}$ | | $\frac{1}{6}$ | | $\frac{1}{6}$ | | $\frac{1}{6}$ | | $\frac{1}{6}$ | | $\frac{1}{6}$ | |

| $\frac{1}{7}$ | $\frac{1}{7}$ | $\frac{1}{7}$ | $\frac{1}{7}$ | $\frac{1}{7}$ | $\frac{1}{7}$ | $\frac{1}{7}$ | | | | | |

| $\frac{1}{8}$ | $\frac{1}{8}$ | $\frac{1}{8}$ | $\frac{1}{8}$ | $\frac{1}{8}$ | $\frac{1}{8}$ | $\frac{1}{8}$ | $\frac{1}{8}$ | | | | |

| $\frac{1}{9}$ | $\frac{1}{9}$ | $\frac{1}{9}$ | $\frac{1}{9}$ | $\frac{1}{9}$ | $\frac{1}{9}$ | $\frac{1}{9}$ | $\frac{1}{9}$ | $\frac{1}{9}$ | | | |

| $\frac{1}{10}$ | $\frac{1}{10}$ | $\frac{1}{10}$ | $\frac{1}{10}$ | $\frac{1}{10}$ | $\frac{1}{10}$ | $\frac{1}{10}$ | $\frac{1}{10}$ | $\frac{1}{10}$ | $\frac{1}{10}$ | | |

| $\frac{1}{11}$ | $\frac{1}{11}$ | $\frac{1}{11}$ | $\frac{1}{11}$ | $\frac{1}{11}$ | $\frac{1}{11}$ | $\frac{1}{11}$ | $\frac{1}{11}$ | $\frac{1}{11}$ | $\frac{1}{11}$ | $\frac{1}{11}$ | |

| $\frac{1}{12}$ | $\frac{1}{12}$ | $\frac{1}{12}$ | $\frac{1}{12}$ | $\frac{1}{12}$ | $\frac{1}{12}$ | $\frac{1}{12}$ | $\frac{1}{12}$ | $\frac{1}{12}$ | $\frac{1}{12}$ | $\frac{1}{12}$ | $\frac{1}{12}$ |

Tangrams

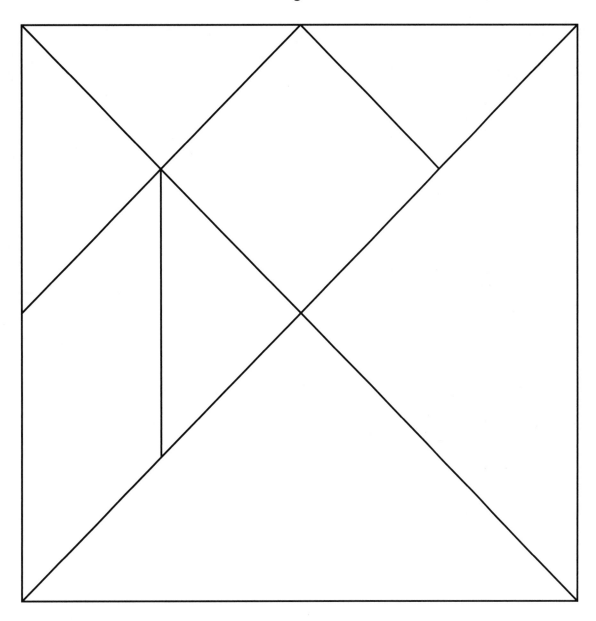